The XXL Soup Maker Recipe Book

Mouthwatering and Easy Meals In Minutes incl. Desserts, Sides and Snacks

Curtis Woodhouse

Copyright © [2022] [Curtis Woodhouse]

All rights reserved

All rights for this book here presented belong exclusively to the author.

Usage or reproduction of the text is forbidden and requires a clear consent of the author in case of expectations.

ISBN - 9798364453143

Table of Contents

Origins Of Soup 7

The Types Of Soup Available 8

How To Create Soup Properly 10

The Soup Making Machine 12

Advantages Of Making Your Own Soup 13

   Vegetable Soup Options 16

      Minestrone Soup 16

      Traditional Tomato Soup 17

      Vegetable Soup 18

      Leek & Potato 19

      Coriander & Carrot Soup 20

      Tomato & Basil Soup 21

      Spinach Soup 22

      Asparagus Soup 23

      Root Vegetable Soup 24

      Pea & Watercress Soup 25

      Courgette, Pea, & Pesto Soup 26

      Green Vegetable Soup 27

   Meat Soups 28

      Leek, Potato and Bacon Soup 28

      Bolognese Soup with Penne 29

      Creamy Chicken and Sweetcorn Soup 30

      Beef Goulash Soup 31

      Lamb and Barley Soup 32

      Pea and Ham Soup 33

      Chicken and Spiced Black Bean Soup 34

      Thai Chicken and Sweet Potato Soup 35

      Chicken Noodle Soup with Peanut Sauce 36

      Lamb and Chickpea Soup 37

      Lemon Chicken Soup 38

      Curried Chicken and Rice Soup 39

Festive Soups 40
    Apple, chestnut, And Butternut Squash Soup 40
    Boxing Day Soup 41
    Christmas Soup 42
    Chestnut, Bacon & Chive Soup 43
    Pumpkin Soup 44
    Czech Christmas Soup 45
    Nutty Pumpkin Delight 46
    Curried Acorn Soup 47
    Butternut & Garlic Soup (works against vampires) 48
    Spring Soup 49
    Mulligatawny Soup 50
    Turkey Noodle Soup 51

Creamy Soups 52
    Ham & Potato Soup 52
    Creamy Chicken & Wild Rice 53
    Creamy Tomato Basil Soup 54
    Creamy Potato & Leek Soup 55
    Chicken Gnocchi Soup 56
    Creamy Tortellini Soup 57
    Cordon Bleu Soup 58
    Creamy Mushroom 59
    Creamy Carrot Soup 60
    Beer Cheese Soup 61
    Irish Parsnip Soup 62

Vegan Soups 63
    Tomato, Chickpea & Pasta Soup 63
    Vegan Noodle Soup 64
    Roast Cauliflower, Cumin & Coconut Milk Soup 65
    Pumpkin, Chilli, & Coconut Soup 66
    Carrot & Ginger Soup 67
    Carrot & Coriander delight 68
    Sweet Potato Soup 69
    Bean & Vegan Pesto Soup 70
    Butternut Squash Soup 71
    Spicy Mexican Bean Soup 73
    Lemongrass & Peppercorn Soup 74
    German Potato Soup 75

Gluten-Free Soups 76
- Minestrone Soup 76
- Carrot & White Bean 77
- Keto Egg Soup 78
- Slow-Cooked Chicken Fajita Soup 79
- Asparagus & Spinach Soup 80
- Sweet & Spicy Carrot Soup 81
- Bean beef Soup 82
- Yellow Split Pea Soup 83
- Chilli Mushroom Soup 84
- Lobster Delight 85
- Cheesy Taco Soup 86
- French Onion Soup 87

Winter Soups 88
- Pesto Minestrone 88
- The Indian Winter 89
- Paprika, Red Pepper & Sweet Potato Soup 91
- Winter Lentil & Vegetable Soup 92
- Ultimate Winter Soup 93
- Winter Vegetable 94
- Hazelnut Truffle Soup 95
- Spicy Root Soup 96
- Cream of Cauliflower 97
- Roasted Carrot And Ginger Soup 98
- Beet Soup 99
- Thai Green Curry Soup 100

Fish Soups 101
- Prawn and Fennel Soup 101
- Haddock and Sweetcorn Soup 102
- Clam Chowder Soup 103
- Spicy Prawn Soup 104
- Sour and Hot Fish Soup 105
- Easy Fish Soup 106

Disclaimer 108

EXCLUSIVE BONUS

40 Weight Loss Recipes

&

14 Days Meal Plan

Scan the QR-Code and receive the FREE download:

Soup is easy to make and can make a delicious meal at any time of the day. It's surprisingly filling and healthy, making it the perfect option for almost any occasion. They aren't just meals, soups are often used as starters and are an effective way to clear your palette between courses.

However, what you may not realize is the sheer number of soups available. Fortunately, this XXL soup maker recipe book will help you to see and sample a wide array of soups.

Prepare to be amazed and have your tastebuds tingling.

Origins Of Soup

The word soup originated in France, it comes from the French word 'soupe', although this is derived from the Latin 'suppa' which meant bread soaked in broth.

Of course, soup is not a new invention, the idea of mixing meats and vegetables in boiling water dates back over 20,000 years. There is evidence of soups being made in 20,000 BC. This isn't surprising as soup is generally a simple meal to create and offers the majority of the nutrients people need every day. It can also be made cheaply with whatever vegetables and meat you have available.

It's worth noting that soup increased dramatically in popularity once waterproof containers were created, the earliest were simple clay containers.

Naturally, soups have evolved alongside the human palette. That's why there is a huge array of flavours available today.

The first dedicated soup shop was opened in Paris in 1765 and soups were marketed as a cure for physical exhaustion. Over the years, soups have become popular across the globe with an array of regional versions.

Of course, soups became even easier to incorporate into busy daily schedules in the 19th century as manufacturers mastered the art of canning. This enabled businesses to manufacturer soups and sell them, allowing consumers to simply reheat and enjoy them.

The soup industry now includes a collection of dried soups, these are exceptionally easy to make and can be taken almost anywhere with you.

While manufactured tinned and dried soups have their place, it's difficult to beat a homemade soup using fresh ingredients. Once you try some of these recipes you'll agree.

The Types Of Soup Available

Soup is generally seen as a starter although it is possible to eat it as a main course, especially if you are only after a light bite.

However, it should be noted that some cultures see soup as a great option between courses, a simple soup can clear the palette, allowing you to enjoy each course.

There are even a few dessert soups. These are mainly served in Asian countries, such as China, Vietnam, and Japan. In some parts of the world, you can find fruit soups, balancing between a meal and a dessert.

But, the majority of soups are designed to be eaten before the meal or instead of it. This includes the increasingly popular cold soup, such as the Spanish gazpacho which is a chilled vegetable soup. Cold soups are generally kept below room temperature.

You'll find there are many different types of soup and the prevalence will depend on where you live in the world. In the UK, vegetable soups are popular, as are meat ones and even fish soups.

There is also an increasing interest in vegetarian/vegan soups and even gluten-free options. Alongside this, there are speciality soups, such as the Boxing Day soup that uses Christmas leftovers.

This recipe book focuses mainly on UK options, allowing you to make the soups with easily obtainable local ingredients. It means you're supporting the local community and enjoying a delicious meal.

You'll find some of the simplest yet tastiest soups in this book, such as minestrone, creamy vegetable, and a delightful chicken noodle soup. The majority of these soups are thicker as this increases the flavour and enjoyment.

Here's a quick list of soup types:

Broth

Broth is a thick soup, much like a stew. It's often made with meat and can be served by itself or as a base for other soups.

Bouillon

Bouillon is a thin soup, usually a broth that has been dehydrated allowing it to be easily made anywhere.

Consommé

This is a thin soup, it's usually clear and watery but should be full of flavour.

Bisque

Bisque is another thick soup generally made with shellfish and alcohol such as wine.

Chowder

Chowder is a thick soup made with seafood, it's thickened with milk or cream.

Creamy

Creamy soups tend to have cream in them and offer a velvet, indulgent, flavour

Velouté

Vegetable or chicken stock-based soups which are thickened with roux.

Cold

Cold soups are deliberately kept below room temperature and served this way.

National soups

These use local ingredients making them distinctive to specific parts of the world.

How To Create Soup Properly

The best way to create high-quality soup is to ensure you have everything in place before you start cooking. This ensures your focus is on the cooking and not on whether you have the right ingredient.

Use local ingredients

The best soups use the freshest ingredients and you can't get fresher than local vegetables. They can be harvested in the morning, bought at your local farmer's market, and made into soup by lunchtime.

Using local ingredients means you're getting the best flavour and maximizing nutritional content.

Prepare everything first

When making soup you'll find it easier to get everything ready first. If the recipe says to crush some garlic cloves and dice some onion, do it before you start the cooking process. It's faster than stopping and starting with vegetable cutting, it also makes the process of creating delicious soup much faster and quicker.

Don't follow the recipe!

The recipe is important, it gives you an idea of what ingredients should be used and how much of them to create a delicious soup. But, that doesn't mean you need to follow it religiously.

It's possible to change the vegetables for the ones you have in your fridge. Or, you can add extra spices and herbs while removing the parts you don't like. If you want to make the best soups possible you mustn't be afraid of turning any recipe into your own creation. That includes adding a little spice.

Don't forget that most soups have stock in them. That means two or three stock cubes in boiling water. The amount of water you use affects the thickness of the soup. The greater the water level the thinner the soup.

It's okay to put less water in and, if the soup is too thick, add some more water later.

Considerations when Choosing Ingredients

As mentioned, the best ingredients are those that are local. That means your soups will follow the seasons, allowing you to make what's easily available today. This is a good option because the fresher the ingredient the higher the nutrient level. While some soups can be extremely high in calories and fats, the majority aren't and are a sensible and nutritious choice. Choosing the right ingredients helps to ensure this is the case.

When looking at ingredients you must check their quality. Just because you're at a farmer's market doesn't mean you will automatically get the highest-quality ingredients. Regardless of where you shop, you need to be feeling and checking each product.

That means observing the colour of the vegetables, their feel of them, and their smell. You'll need to trust your judgement, if you have any doubts then choose a different vegetable.

Don't forget to check your own supplies. In most cases, it is easy to swap an ingredient or two and still make a delicious soup. So, if you have parsnips at home, use them instead of carrots or pick a different recipe. There is no sense in letting the vegetables you already have go to waste.

The Soup Making Machine

The recipes in this book are mainly created on the top of your oven, a few use a slow cooker or a Dutch oven but all can be done on your hob. This allows you to monitor the process and tweak the soup as needed. However, mixing and cooking the ingredients yourself is not your only option.

It is possible to get a soup-making machine, it can be a good investment if you make a lot of soups.

These machines are all different but the basic design principle is the same. A soup maker has a built-in heater. This allows it to cook the soup in the same way that you can in a slow cooker or on the hob.

All you have to do is put your ingredients in the machine and set it for the amount of time and temperature you desire. As it cooks blades inside the machine turn and keep mixing all the ingredients. The more expensive soup makers also incorporated thermos-style insulation, keeping your soup hotter for longer.

It should be noted that the key to great soup is making sure the vegetables are cooked properly. In general, the smaller the piece of vegetable the easier it is for it to soften. Although you can set the size of the pieces in your machine, it pays to cut them to approximately the right size before you introduce them to your soup maker.

Doing this ensures they cook properly and your soup maker does the job perfectly.

Don't forget, all soup makers are different and you should read the instructions pertaining to yours before you use it for the first time. There are often special features that can benefit you when cooking.

Advantages Of Making Your Own Soup

If you're wondering why you should bother making your own soup instead of buying ready-made soup then wonder no more!

Dietary control

The majority of processed foods, including pre-prepared soups, have high levels of sugar and salt. These, along with a collection of chemicals, help the soup taste great, make you want to eat it again, and preserve the lifespan of the soup.

Unfortunately, high salt levels and chemicals in food, specifically in processed foods, have been linked with an increased risk of age-related diseases.

If you want to maintain your maximum health it's better to make your own soups. Then you know what is in them.

Weight loss

The same is true if you're looking to lose weight. Choosing soup can seem like a good idea but, as mentioned, processed soups have high levels of sugar and salt in them. The sugar is likely to increase any weight issues you have, not decrease them.

By choosing to make the soups yourself you can avoid anything other than natural ingredients, effectively ensuring you're getting important nutrients while losing weight.

Cost-saving

It may seem cost-effective to grab a can of soup from the store but it's unlikely to be as cheap as creating your own soup. More importantly, if you're heading to the store to get something to eat, you'll probably end up choosing something other than soup. That makes the cost even higher and the idea of creating your own soup far more financially attractive.

Advance Planning

One of the biggest problems most people face is a lack of time. There are so many things to do every day it can be hard to find the time to cook healthy meals. That's why it's easier to live on processed foods.

But, if you make your own soups, you can make them in bulk, essentially making meals to enjoy during the week. It takes very little time and effort but means you always have a healthy option at home.

This type of planning can make sure you eat healthier and save you money. What better reason do you need to start looking through this impressive collection of soup recipes?

EXCLUSIVE BONUS

40 Weight Loss Recipes

&

14 Days Meal Plan

Scan the QR-Code and receive the FREE download:

VEGETABLE SOUP OPTIONS

Minestrone Soup

SERVES 6
PREP TIME: 15 MINUTES | TOTAL: 65 MINUTES
NET CARBS: 22G | PROTEIN: 9G | FIBRE: 7G | FAT: 10G
KCAL: 225

Ingredients
- 1 onion – chopped into small pieces
- 1 piece of celery – also chopped
- 1 carrot – peeled then chopped
- 1 courgette - chopped
- 70g pancetta – finely chopped
- 70g pasta
- 3 tbsp olive oil
- 1 crushed garlic clove
- 1 tin cannellini beans (400g)
- 1 tin chopped tomatoes (400g)
- 2 tbsp tomato puree
- 1 litre vegetable stock

Instructions
1. Start by warming the oil in a pan
2. Add the onion, celery, carrot, courgette, and pancetta. Cook for ten minutes until lightly browned
3. Put the crushed garlic and any herbs you wish into the pan and cook for another minute
4. Mix in beans, chopped tomatoes, puree, and the stock
5. Add salt and pepper to taste – if desired (or anything else you wish to adjust the flavour with)
6. Simmer the ingredients for 30 minutes
7. Drop the pasta in and let it simmer for another 10 minutes
8. Serve with the garnish of your choice and enjoy

Top Tip: Goes well with freshly baked bread

Traditional Tomato Soup

SERVES 4
PREP TIME: 45 MINUTES | TOTAL: 90 MINUTES
NET CARBS: 13G | PROTEIN: 4G | FIBRE: 4G | FAT: 7G
KCAL: 123

Ingredients
- 1250g of fresh ripe tomatoes
- 1 onion
- 1 carrot
- 1 piece of celery
- Pinch of sugar
- 2 tbsp olive oil
- 1 tbsp tomato puree
- 1.2 litres of vegetable stock (2 stock cubes in boiling water)

Instructions
1. Take your tomatoes and check there are no green bits attached to them
2. Wash the tomatoes and cut them into quarters. Remove any hard cores. If you don't, they won't suffer and give you uncomfortable hard bits in your soup
3. Peel your onion and carrot before finely dicing them
4. Chop your celery stick into small pieces
5. Put the olive oil in a pan and warm it slowly
6. Once the oil is warm add your carrot, celery, and onion
7. Mix thoroughly and cook for 10 minutes
8. You can now add the tomato puree and the tomatoes
9. Add the sugar and any salt or pepper you wish
10. Keep the pan on moderate heat and let everything simmer for 10 minutes
11. Add your already hot broth and bring it all to the boil while stirring
12. Turn the heat down low and put a lid on the pan
13. Leave it to stew for 25 minutes – you may want to stir it occasionally
14. Put the mixture into a blender and blend until smooth – should take 30-60 seconds
15. Reheat the soup in the original pan before serving it with desired garnish

Vegetable Soup

SERVES 4
PREP TIME: 10 MINUTES | TOTAL: 40 MINUTES
NET CARBS: 44G | PROTEIN: 10G | FIBRE: 6G | FAT: 11G
KCAL: 325

Ingredients
- 200g sourdough bread – you'll need to cut this into crouton-sized pieces
- 1 garlic clove finely diced
- 100g cherry tomatoes
- 1 can chopped tomatoes (400g)
- 1 potato – chopped into small pieces
- 1 carrot – also chopped
- 1 piece of celery – chopped into small pieces
- A handful of caraway seeds
- 150g shredded white cabbage
- 200g cauliflower – break it into individual florets
- Pinch of sugar to taste
- Herbs as desired
- 2 tbsp olive oil

Instructions
1. Start by heating your oven to 180°C (160°C if you have a fan oven)
2. Spread the cut bread on a tray sprinkled with caraway seeds and drizzled with a little olive oil
3. Cook in the oven for 15 minutes
4. Heat a tablespoon of olive oil in a pan until warm
5. Add potato, garlic, and carrot and heat until softened. That should take 5 minutes
6. Mix the stock into the pan then, as it starts to simmer, add the tomatoes, celery, and sugar
7. Cook for ten minutes then mix in the cauliflower and cabbage
8. Cook for another 15 minutes
9. Dish into soup bowls and add the croutons to each bowl

Leek & Potato

SERVES 6
PREP TIME: 20 MINUTES | TOTAL: 45 MINUTES
NET CARBS: 18G | PROTEIN: 5G | FIBRE: 3G | FAT: 18G
KCAL:252

Ingredients
- 450g potatoes – peel them and cut them into small pieces
- 1 onion – chopped into small pieces
- 450g leeks – slice them finely
- 50g butter or equivalent spread
- 1l litres of vegetable stock
- 125ml milk – preferably full-fat
- 1 small carton whipping cream (approx. 140ml)

Instructions
1. Start by putting the butter in a pan and heating it on the stove
2. Once melted add the potatoes, onion, and leek
3. Make sure they are well coated in the butter as they simmer
4. Add some salt and pepper if desired
5. Add a piece of greaseproof paper to the pan, above the vegetables
6. Place the lid on and leave it on low heat for 10 minutes
7. Pour your stock in then bring the mixture to the boil and simmer for another 5 minutes
8. Blend the soup in your blender to ensure it is smooth
9. Reheat in the original pan to ensure it is piping hot
10. Add the whipping cream and milk and simmer for a few more minutes
11. Serve with your choice of fresh bread and garnish

Coriander & Carrot Soup

SERVES 4
PREP TIME: 15 MINUTES | TOTAL: 40 MINUTES
NET CARBS: 19G | PROTEIN: 3G | FIBRE: 5G | FAT: 4G
KCAL:115

Ingredients
- 1 medium-sized onion finely chopped
- 1 potato peeled and chopped into small pieces
- 450g carrots – also peeled and chopped into small pieces
- 1 tbsp olive oil
- 1.2 litres of vegetable stock
- Ground herbs if desired

Instructions
1. Put the chopped onion in a pan with the olive oil and heat on the stove
2. It should take 5 minutes for the onion to soften
3. Add the potato and continue heating for another minute
4. Pour in the carrots and vegetable stock, and mix thoroughly
5. Bring the mixture to the boil then turn the heat down, allowing it to simmer
6. Cover your saucepan and leave it for 20 minutes
7. Add any desired herbs and pour the soup into your blender
8. It should take 30-60 seconds to make it smooth
9. Put it back into your pan and reheat
10. Taste test and adjust with herbs or salt and pepper before serving
11. Enjoy!

Tomato & Basil Soup

SERVES 4
PREP TIME: 10 MINUTES | TOTAL: 25 MINUTES
NET CARBS: 14G | PROTEIN: 8G | FIBRE: 4G | FAT: 14G
KCAL: 213

Ingredients
- 2 cloves of garlic – you can crush these
- 3 tins plum tomatoes (tins of 400g each)
- ½ litre vegetable stock
- 5 sundried tomatoes – chopped into large pieces
- 1 tbsp olive oil – you can use any vegetable oil you want
- Pinch sugar
- 125g basil pesto
- A small pot of soured cream (around 140ml)
- Additional herbs and salt/pepper as desired

Instructions
1. Start by putting the oil into a saucepan and allowing it to melt on a low heat
2. Add the crushed garlic, plum tomatoes, sundried tomato pieces and sugar to your pan
3. Allow it to warm and, when it reaches a simmer, add the vegetable stock
4. Keep it on low heat and let it simmer for 10 minutes, stirring occasionally
5. Remove the pan from the heat and slowly add the cream while whisking the soup – it's best to use an electric whisk for this
6. Add extra sugar if you wish
7. Return to the heat for a few minutes to ensure the soup is piping hot
8. Pour it into bowls and then pour a quarter of the basil pesto on top of each bowl
9. Add basil leaves if desired

Spinach Soup

SERVES 4
PREP TIME: 10 MINUTES | TOTAL: 35 MINUTES
NET CARBS: 13G | PROTEIN: 6G | FIBRE: 5G | FAT: 13G
KCAL:192

Ingredients

- 1 reasonable size bunch of spring onions – finely chopped
- 25g butter or equivalent spread
- 1 potato – needs to be peeled and cut into small pieces
- 1 leek – also sliced into small sections
- 1 large piece of celery or several small pieces diced
- 1 litre vegetable stock
- 400g spinach – finely chopped
- 150g crème fraiche – can be half or full fat

Instructions

1. As with most soups, start by heating your butter in a pan over a stove on low heat
2. Once melted add the chopped leek, onion, celery, and potato, and stir thoroughly
3. Cover the pan and leave the vegetables to simmer for ten minutes
4. Drop the spinach into the pan and stir continuously for two minutes
5. Once the spinach has wilted pour the contents into a blender and blend until smooth – it could take a couple of minutes
6. Put it back into the pan and add your crème fraiche
7. Warm the soup on the stove until hot
8. Serve straight away
9. Add some freshly baked bread to perfectly finish it

Asparagus Soup

SERVES 4
PREP TIME: 10 MINUTES | TOTAL: 30 MINUTES
NET CARBS: 6G | PROTEIN: 4G | FIBRE: 4G | FAT: 8G
KCAL:101

Ingredients
- 350g asparagus – weight should be after removing the ends
- 1 medium onion finely chopped
- 2 cloves of garlic crushed
- 100g spinach
- 25g butter
- Drizzle of olive oil
- 700ml vegetable stock
- Freshly baked or purchased bread, if desired

Instructions
1. Warm your 25g of butter in a pan and allow it to fully melt
2. Chop the asparagus and drop it into the pan
3. Heat for a few minutes until soft, remove the asparagus from the pan and put them in a bowl for later
4. Place the onion and garlic in the pan and allow them to simmer for 5 minutes
5. Add the asparagus back in and simmer for another 5 minutes
6. Pour in the vegetable stock and the spinach
7. Bring the mixture to the boil, stirring constantly
8. Transfer it to your blender and blend until the mixture is smooth
9. Put it back in the pan and reheat to ensure it is hot
10. Add salt or pepper to taste, if desired
11. Serve in bowls and garnish with herbs of your choice
12. Add the fresh bread, if you have it

Root Vegetable Soup

SERVES 4
PREP TIME: 10 MINUTES | TOTAL: 45 MINUTES
NET CARBS: 56G | PROTEIN: 15G | FIBRE: 9G | FAT: 14G
KCAL:387

Ingredients
- 2 onions – peeled and chopped small
- 2 sweet potatoes – also chopped into small pieces
- 2 carrots - finely chopped
- 2 parsnips – finely chopped
- 2 tbsp olive oil – or your preferred oil
- 75g dried lentils – preferably green
- 1 red chilli pepper – chopped into medium-sized pieces
- Pinch ground cumin

Instructions
1. Put the olive oil into a suitable pan and warm it on a stove, keeping the heat low
2. Add the onions to the pan and heat for 5 minutes, tossing regularly
3. Add the rest of the vegetables and keep the pan on the heat for at least another 5 minutes, until they start browning
4. Cook for a further two minutes while stirring in the cumin and red chilli
5. Now pour the stock into your mixture and the lentils
6. Bring the mixture to the boil, stirring to stop it from sticking and burning
7. Lower the heat and leave it to simmer for 25 minutes
8. Pour it into the blender and blend until smooth
9. Put it back in the pan to reheat before serving
10. A good serving suggestion is to add a drop of Greek yoghurt to each bowl and a little coriander

Pea & Watercress Soup

SERVES 4
PREP TIME: 5 MINUTES | TOTAL: 20 MINUTES
NET CARBS: 17G | PROTEIN: 18G | FIBRE: 5G | FAT: 18G
KCAL: 256

Ingredients
- 1 medium size onion chopped into small pieces
- 1 garlic clove – chopped small
- 1 potato peeled and cut roughly into chunks
- 1 tbsp olive oil
- 300g fresh peas – you can use frozen if you wish
- 1100g watercress
- 100ml double cream
- 500ml of vegetable stock

Instructions
1. Start by warming the oil in your saucepan, and keep the heat on low
2. Add the onion and garlic and cook for 5 minutes, it should be enough to soften it
3. Pour in the vegetable stock and the pieces of potato
4. Bring to the boil and allow the mixture to simmer for 7-10 minutes
5. Add your watercress and peas, bring the mixture back to the boil and simmer for another 3 minutes. It's best to cover the pan during this stage
6. Pour the soup into your blender and blend until smooth
7. Put it back in the pan and heat to make sure it's hot
8. While heating add the cream and any salt/pepper you want
9. Serve, ideally with a mint leaf or two on top

Courgette, Pea, & Pesto Soup

SERVES 4
PREP TIME: 10 MINUTES | TOTAL: 25 MINUTES
NET CARBS: 19G | PROTEIN: 10G | FIBRE: 9G | FAT: 8G
KCAL:206

Ingredients
- 1 clove of garlic finely sliced
- 200g fresh or frozen peas
- 500g courgettes – cut the ends off and slice them lengthways into quarters
- 1 can (400g) of cannellini beans
- 1l vegetable stock (2 vegetable stock cubes melted in water)
- 2 tbsp basil pesto
- 1 tbsp olive oil

Instructions
1. Pour the olive oil into your pan and warm it up on the stove
2. Add the garlic and heat gently for several seconds
3. Tip the courgette pieces in and cook for three minutes, stirring regularly
4. Add your peas and cannellini beans
5. Pour in the vegetable stock and allow the mixture to simmer for 3-5 minutes
6. Add the pesto and heat for another 1-2 minutes
7. Transfer it to bowls and serve immediately
8. Add fresh brown bread to bring out the flavour

Green Vegetable Soup

SERVES 6
PREP TIME: 10 MINUTES | TOTAL: 25 MINUTES
NET CARBS: 16G | PROTEIN: 7G | FIBRE: 4G | FAT: 3G
KCAL:127

Ingredients
- 1 potato peeled and chopped into small chunks
- 1 large bunch of spring onions – finely chopped
- 1 crushed clove of garlic
- 1l vegetable stock
- 250g frozen peas
- 100g fresh spinach
- 300ml plain yoghurt

Instructions
1. Grab a pan and add your potato, spring onions, and garlic.
2. Turn the heat on and add the vegetable stock
3. Slowly, while stirring, bring the mixture to the boil
4. Turn the heat down to allow the mixture to simmer
5. Add a lid to the pan and leave it on the heat for 15 minutes
6. Remove the lid and pour the peas in
7. Turn the heat up to ensure the soup reaches boiling point again
8. Add the yoghurt and spinach, stir thoroughly
9. Transfer the mixture to your blender and blend until it's smooth
10. Put it back in the pan and add salt and pepper to taste, if desired
11. Reheat then serve with a garnish of your choice

MEAT SOUPS

Leek, Potato and Bacon Soup

SERVES 4-6
PREP TIME: 30 MINUTES | TOTAL: 30 MINUTES
NET CARBS: 15G | PROTEIN: 6G | FIBRE: 4G | FAT: 11 G
KCAL: 175

Ingredients
- 25g butter
- 3 rashers bacon
- 1 chopped onion
- 400g sliced leeks
- 3 medium-sized potatoes – peeled and diced
- 1.4 litres of hot vegetable stock
- 142ml single cream

Instructions
1. Melt the butter in a large saucepan
2. Pour in the bacon and onions and stir until they start to turn golden
3. Add the leeks and potatoes
4. Stir the mixture well and cover
5. Turn down the heat and cook slowly for five minutes
6. Add the vegetable stock and bring the mixture to the boil
7. Cover and simmer for twenty minutes
8. Turn off the heat and leave the mixture to cool
9. Blend the mixture in a food processor until smooth
10. Return the blended mixture to the saucepan and add the cream
11. Taste and season if necessary

Bolognese Soup with Penne

SERVES 4
PREP TIME: 10 MINUTES | TOTAL: 35 MINUTES
NET CARBS: 35G | PROTEIN: 24G | FIBRE: 9G | FAT: 9G
KCAL: 337

Ingredients
- 3 finely chopped onions
- 3 large chopped carrots
- 2 finely chopped celery sticks
- 3 chopped garlic cloves
- 2 teaspoons rapeseed oil
- 250g 5% steak mince
- 500g passata
- 1 tablespoon vegetable bouillon powder
- 100g wholemeal penne
- 1 teaspoon paprika
- 4 sprigs thyme
- 45g grated parmesan

Instructions
1. Heat the oil in a large pan
2. Fry the onions for a few minutes until soft
3. Pour in the carrots, celery and garlic and fry for five minutes
4. Add the mince and stir well until brown
5. Pour in the passata and bouillon with 1.3 litres of boiling water
6. Add the thyme and paprika to the mixture
7. Cover the pan, and simmer for fifteen minutes
8. Pour in the penne and cook for approximately fifteen minutes until tender
9. Add the grated parmesan and stir well

Creamy Chicken and Sweetcorn Soup

SERVES 4
PREP TIME: 25 MINUTES | TOTAL: 50 MINUTES
NET CARBS: 15G | PROTEIN: 26G | FIBRE: 4G | FAT: 15G
KCAL: 303

Ingredients
- 1 celery stick
- 1 sliced leek
- 300ml chicken stock
- 250g sweetcorn (crush half lightly with a fork)
- 200g finely sliced greens (spinach or kale)
- Small bunch of chives
- 2 x 1 tablespoon olive oil
- 25g butter
- 25g plain flour
- 250ml milk
- 2/3 skinless chicken thigh fillets cut into cubes
- 1 skinless chicken breast cut into cubes
- 1/3 finely chopped onion

Instructions
1. Melt the butter in a saucepan and stir in the flour
2. Carefully pour in the milk whisking continuously
3. Leave the mixture to simmer, stirring regularly until it thickens
4. Heat 1 tablespoon of oil in a pan, and add the chicken until it starts to colour at the edges
5. Remove the chicken pieces and place them on a plate
6. Tip the onion into the pan and cook until soft
7. Add the chicken pieces, onions and any juices to the white sauce mixture
8. Mix well and cook for fifteen minutes until the chicken is thoroughly cooked
9. Put to one side
10. Heat the remaining tablespoon of oil in a pan
11. Tip in the celery and leek, and fry until soft
12. Pour in the white sauce mixture and stock
13. Stir well and bring the mixture to a simmer
14. Finally, add the sweetcorn and stir in the greens
15. Sprinkle with finely chopped chives and serve

Beef Goulash Soup

SERVES 2-3
PREP TIME: 15 MINUTES | TOTAL: 60 MINUTES
NET CARBS: 28G | PROTEIN: 25G | FIBRE: 7G | FAT: 12G
KCAL: 345

Ingredients
- 1 large onion sliced
- 3 sliced garlic cloves
- 1 tablespoon rapeseed oil
- 200g lean stewing beef
- 1 teaspoon caraway seeds
- 2 teaspoons paprika
- 400g tin chopped tomatoes
- 600ml beef stock
- 1 medium sweet potato peeled and diced
- 1 green pepper diced
- 150g natural bio yoghurt
- Chopped parsley

Instructions
1. Heat the oil in a pan
2. Add the garlic and onion, and fry for five minutes
3. Tip in the beef and increase the heat
4. Stir well until the beef starts to brown
5. Add the paprika, caraway seeds, tomatoes and stock
6. Stir well and cover
7. Leave to simmer for thirty minutes
8. Stir in the diced sweet potato and green pepper
9. Cover the pan and cook for a further twenty minutes
10. Serve topped with natural yoghurt and parsley

Lamb and Barley Soup

SERVES 4
PREP TIME: 10 MINUTES | TOTAL: 25 MINUTES
NET CARBS: 26G | PROTEIN:17 G | FIBRE:4 G | FAT:11 G
KCAL: 258

Ingredients
- 200g lamb neck fillet (remove the fat and cut into small pieces)
- ½ onion chopped finely
- 1 teaspoon olive oil
- 50g pearl barley
- 600g of various root vegetables
- 1 litre lamb or beef stock
- 100g green beans finely chopped
- 1 sprig of thyme
- 2 teaspoons Worcestershire sauce

Instructions
1. Heat the oil in a pan
2. Add the lamb pieces and fry for several minutes until browned
3. Tip in the onion and barley, and fry for a further minute
4. Pour in the vegetables, and cook for another two minutes
5. Pour in the stock and add the Worcestershire sauce and thyme
6. Cover the pan and simmer for twenty minutes
7. Remove approximately ¼ of the mixture and blend
8. Pour the blended mixture back into the original pan
9. Add the green beans and simmer for three minutes
10. Serve with warm bread

Pea and Ham Soup

SERVES 4
PREP TIME: 10 MINUTES | TOTAL: 15 MINUTES
NET CARBS: 18.3G | PROTEIN: 28.5G | FIBRE: 7.3G | FAT: 6.3G
KCAL: 243

Ingredients
- 1 chopped onion
- 1 medium-sized potato – peeled and chopped
- 1 litre of ham or pork stock
- 500g frozen petit pois
- 300g thick sliced ham (remove any fat and chop into pieces)
- 1 knob of butter

Instructions
1. Melt the knob of butter and add the chopped onion
2. Cook until the onion has softened
3. Add the chopped potato and stir well
4. Pour in the 1 litre of stock
5. Simmer until the potato has softened
6. Tip in the 500g petit pois and bring to the boil
7. Remove the pan from the heat and blend until smooth
8. Add the remaining 300g chopped ham, and stir well
9. Season and serve

Chicken and Spiced Black Bean Soup

SERVES 4
PREP TIME: 10 MINUTES | TOTAL: 15 MINUTES
NET CARBS: 15G | PROTEIN: 26G | FIBRE: 6G | FAT: 11G
KCAL: 293

Ingredients
- 2 crushed garlic cloves
- 2 tbsp olive oil
- Finely chopped coriander stalks
- Zest 1 lime and cut into wedges
- 2 teaspoons cumin
- 1 teaspoon chilli flakes
- 400g tin chopped tomatoes
- 400g tin black beans (rinsed and drained)
- 600ml chicken stock
- 175g kale (remove the thick stalks and shred the leaves)
- 250g leftover roast chicken or ready-cooked chicken
- 50g feta
- Flour and corn tortillas – toasted to serve

Instructions
1. Heat the oil in a large pan
2. Add the crushed garlic, coriander stalks and lime zest, and fry for two minutes
3. Tip in the cumin and chilli flakes, and fry for a further minute
4. Pour in the tinned tomatoes, black beans and stock
5. Bring to the boil
6. Using a potato masher crush the beans against the bottom of the saucepan
7. Add the kale, and simmer for five minutes
8. Tip in the chicken and season well
9. Add juice from half the lime
10. Serve and sprinkle the feta on top

Thai Chicken and Sweet Potato Soup

SERVES 2
PREP TIME: 5 MINUTES | TOTAL: 30 MINUTES
NET CARBS: 30G | PROTEIN: 19.2G | FIBRE: 3.2G | FAT: 18.1G
KCAL: 360

Ingredients
- 2 chopped garlic cloves
- 1 deseeded and chopped red chilli
- 2cm piece chopped root ginger
- 1 lemongrass stalk (bashed)
- 25g coriander (chop leaves and stalks separately)
- 1 teaspoon olive oil
- 2 tbsp red Thai curry paste
- 750ml chicken stock
- 160ml coconut cream
- 500g sweet potato – peeled and chopped
- 2 sliced skinless chicken breasts
- Juice of 1 lime
- ½ teaspoon fish sauce
- 1 teaspoon sugar

Instructions
1. Heat the oil in a large saucepan
2. Add the garlic, lemongrass, ginger, chilli, coriander stalks and curry paste
3. Cook for approximately three minutes
4. Pour in the chicken stock, coconut cream and sweet potatoes
5. Cook for fifteen minutes until soft
6. Remove the lemongrass and throw it away
7. Tip the mixture into a blender, and blend until smooth
8. Return the blended mixture to the saucepan
9. Add the chicken and cook on low heat for around ten minutes
10. Pour in the lime juice, sugar and fish sauce
11. Sprinkle the coriander leaves and serve

Chicken Noodle Soup with Peanut Sauce

SERVES 2
PREP TIME: 15 MINUTES | TOTAL: 30 MINUTES
NET CARBS: 25G | PROTEIN: 48G | FIBRE: 6G | FAT:14 G
KCAL: 434

Ingredients
- 1 tablespoon sunflower oil
- 4 skinless and boneless chicken thighs
- 1 crushed garlic clove
- 1 small piece of ginger (grated)
- 500ml chicken stock
- 1 teaspoon soy sauce
- ½ cabbage sliced
- 150g mushrooms
- 150g straight-to-wok noodles
- 1 tablespoon peanut butter
- 1 teaspoon soy sauce
- 1 teaspoon honey

Instructions
1. Heat the oil in a large pan
2. Tip in the chicken and brown
3. Add the crushed garlic and ginger, stir well
4. Pour in the chicken stock and 1 teaspoon of soy sauce
5. Bring the mixture to the boil and reduce it to a simmer
6. Cover the pan with a lid and simmer for 30 minutes
7. In a bowl add the peanut butter, soy sauce and honey, mix well
8. Put the bowl to one side
9. Lift the chicken out of the pan and shred it on a plate
10. Tip in the cabbage, mushrooms and noodles to the pan
11. Turn up the heat
12. Add the shredded chicken, and stir well
13. Ladle into bowls and drizzle with the peanut mixture

Lamb and Chickpea Soup

SERVES 2
PREP TIME: 15 MINUTES | TOTAL: 40 MINUTES
NET CARBS: 37G | PROTEIN: 27G | FIBRE: 20G | FAT: 15G
KCAL: 430

Ingredients
- 1 tablespoon olive oil
- 1 sliced onion
- 3 chopped celery sticks
- 125g lean lamb leg steak – fat trimmed off and cut into small pieces
- 2 diced carrots
- 1 teaspoon ground turmeric
- 1 teaspoon cumin
- 1 teaspoon coriander
- 400g tin green lentils
- 210g tin chickpeas
- 2 tbsp tomato puree
- 2 teaspoons vegetable bouillon powder
- ½ small bunch of parsley chopped finely

Instructions
1. Heat the oil in a large deep pan
2. Add the diced carrots, sliced onion and chopped celery
3. Cook on high heat, stirring regularly
4. Tip in the lamb pieces and spices
5. Cook for approximately seven minutes to brown the lamb
6. Pour in the tin of lentils and chickpeas
7. Mix in the tomato puree, bouillon powder and add 1 litre of hot water
8. Bring the mixture to a boil
9. Cover the pan and simmer for thirty minutes
10. Stir in the chopped parsley and serve

Lemon Chicken Soup

SERVES 4
PREP TIME: 10 MINUTES | TOTAL: 30 MINUTES
NET CARBS: 25G | PROTEIN: 27G | FIBRE: 3G | FAT: 17G
KCAL: 364

Ingredients

- 1 tablespoon rapeseed oil
- 2 large leeks finely sliced
- 2 finely chopped celery stalks
- 1.5 litres of chicken stock
- 100g risotto rice
- 300g leftover roast chicken shredded
- 2 whisked eggs
- 2 lemons juiced

Instructions

1. Heat the oil in a large pan
2. Tip in the leeks and celery, and fry for ten minutes
3. Pour in the chicken stock and bring to the boil
4. Add the risotto rice and shredded chicken
5. Turn down the heat and simmer for twenty minutes
6. Remove the pan from the heat and leave to cool for fifteen minutes
7. Rapidly whisk in the eggs and lemon juice until the mixture is creamy
8. Spoon into bowls and serve

Curried Chicken and Rice Soup

SERVES 4
PREP TIME: 20 MINUTES | TOTAL: 35 MINUTES
NET CARBS: 38G | PROTEIN: 38G | FIBRE: 5G | FAT: 41G
KCAL: 679

Ingredients
- 2 tbsp oil - your preferred type
- 1 finely chopped onion
- 3 tbsp curry paste
- 800ml of coconut milk
- 400ml hot water with two stock cubes
- 4 eggs
- 30g leftover cooked chicken torn into small pieces
- 100g rice of your choice – preferably risotto
- 1 tin sweetcorn
- 3 tbsp lime juice
- 2 sliced spring onions

Instructions
1. Put the oil in a pan over a medium heat
2. Add the chopped onion and cook for ten minutes
3. Tip in the curry paste, stir, stir while simmering for one minute
4. Pour in the milk, once mixed add your stock, followed by your choice of rice
5. Bring the mixture to the boil then reduce the heat and cook for twenty minutes
6. Separately heat a pan of water
7. Drop the eggs into the water and leave for seven minutes
8. Tip in the shredded chicken and sweetcorn
9. Stir well and cook for five minutes
10. Season the mixture well before adding your lime juice
11. Deshell the eggs and section them into quarters
12. Layer the soup with your freshly cooked eggs and spread the spring onion across the top

FESTIVE SOUPS

Apple, chestnut, And Butternut Squash Soup

SERVES 8
PREP TIME: 30 MINUTES | TOTAL: 1HR 30 MINUTES
NET CARBS: 46G | PROTEIN: 13G | FIBRE: 9G | FAT: 18G
KCAL:354

Ingredients
- 1 ½kg butternut squash – remove the seeds then cut into large chunks
- 5 tbsp olive oil
- 1 onion, peeled then finely sliced
- 2 potatoes, peeled and cut into cubes
- 1 clove of garlic diced
- 2 apples, peeled and then cut into small pieces
- 500g roasted chestnuts, peeled and sliced
- Little fresh thyme
- 400g chestnut puree
- 2 litres of vegetable stock

Instructions
1. Start by heating your oven. Set the temp to 200°C (gas mark 6)
2. Cover the butternut squash chunks with olive oil and spread them across a baking sheet
3. Put the tray in the oven and cook for 25-30 minutes, the butternut should be tender
4. Allow the butternut squash to cool then you'll easily be able to remove the skin with your fingers
5. Put a tablespoon of olive oil in a pan and add the garlic, apple pieces, and potato cubes
6. Warm on the hob, allowing the items to cook for 3-5 minutes. You want them soft not browned
7. Tip in your vegetable stock and your butternut squash
8. While bringing the soup to boiling add the thyme, chestnuts, and chestnut puree
9. Allow to simmer for 20 minutes
10. Put the soup into your blender and blend for 2-3 minutes, until smooth
11. Serve, or if needed, reheat on the hob before serving

Boxing Day Soup

SERVES 4
PREP TIME: 15 MINUTES | TOTAL: 45 MINUTES
NET CARBS: 31G | PROTEIN: 8G | FIBRE: 8G | FAT: 6G
KCAL: 214

Ingredients
- 1 Tbsp olive oil
- 1 onion, peeled and finely sliced
- 2 pieces of celery – thinly sliced
- 2 potatoes, peeled and cubed
- 1.2 litres of vegetable stock
- 550g leftover Christmas vegetables
- 1 tbsp curry paste or powder
- Salt and pepper if desired

Instructions
1. Put a pan on the hob and turn it on to a medium heat
2. Add the olive oil and, once warm, slide in the onion
3. Cook for 5 minutes until soft then add the celery
4. Cook for another 5 minutes before adding potato cubes and cooking for another 2 minutes
5. Now add the vegetable stock and curry paste/powder
6. Bring the mixture to the boil and reduce the heat
7. Cover and allow it to simmer for 20 minutes
8. Place your leftover Christmas veg into the mix and continue heating for 3-5 minutes
9. If you wish you can transfer it to a blender and blend it to obtain a smooth soup, but it's not essential
10. You're ready to serve, add some plain yoghurt or crème fraiche as a garnish

Christmas Soup

SERVES 6
PREP TIME: 5 MINUTES | TOTAL: 2HR 5 MINUTES
NET CARBS: 47G | PROTEIN: 12G | FIBRE: 9G | FAT: 18G
KCAL:498

Ingredients
- 2 x 400g tins of chopped tomatoes
- 10 fresh tomatoes, chopped into sections
- 2 green chillies, seeded and finely sliced
- 500g cheddar cheese, or your preferred option
- S500ml vegetable stock
- 200ml sour cream
- 1 packet of pasta
- Pinch red pepper flakes
- 1 tbsp fresh basil, diced

Instructions
1. You can use a standard pan or a slow cooker for this festive soup
2. Add the tomatoes and green chillies to your pot with the cheese and vegetable stock
3. Bring the mixture to the boil and reduce the heat
4. Allow it to simmer for 30 minutes
5. Separately, cook your pasta according to the instructions on the packet, you want it to be firm, (al dente)
6. Lower the heat under the tomatoes and stir in the sour cream
7. Now add the cooked pasta, red pepper flakes, and thyme
8. Let the soup simmer for an hour
9. Check the taste and add any seasoning if required
10. Serve and enjoy. If desired swirl some cream or yoghurt on the top of each serving

Chestnut, Bacon & Chive Soup

SERVES 8
PREP TIME: 30 MINUTES | TOTAL: 60 MINUTES
NET CARBS: 38G | PROTEIN: 12G | FIBRE: 5G | FAT: 16G
KCAL: 324

Ingredients
- 1 tbsp olive oil
- 4 slices bacon cut into small pieces
- 1 carrot, topped and tailed then finely sliced
- 1 piece of celery cut into strips
- 1 leek, split lengthways then cut into small strips
- 1 onion, peeled and chopped
- 600ml vegetable stock
- 200g roasted chestnuts
- 100ml cream
- Salt and pepper as desired

Instructions
1. Put a pan over medium heat on the hob and add the olive oil
2. Once warm, add the bacon pieces and fry until they start to crisp, that should be 8-10 minutes
3. Remove the bacon and place it on some kitchen towel to absorb excess fat
4. Put the onion, leek, carrot, and celery into the still-warm pan and cook for 10 minutes
5. Keep the medium heat as you add the chestnuts, then the stock, and stir
6. Allow the soup to come to the boil, reduce the heat, and let it simmer for 30 minutes
7. Transfer to your blender and blend until it's smooth
8. Put it back into the pan to reheat
9. While heating add the bacon pieces and cream while stirring, it should be thick and creamy
10. Serve with your choice of garnish

Pumpkin Soup

SERVES 8
PREP TIME: 15 MINUTES | TOTAL: 1HR 15 MINUTES
NET CARBS: 26G | PROTEIN: 11G | FIBRE: 11G | FAT: 8G
KCAL:242

Ingredients
- 750ml vegetable stock
- 1 pumpkin, deseeded with innards removed and pureed
- 2 onions, peeled and finely chopped
- 1 garlic clove crushed
- Pinch of fresh parsley
- 4 tbsp whipping cream
- Pinch of thyme
- Salt and pepper to taste

Instructions
1. Put the vegetable stock in a pan and warm over the hob on a medium heat
2. Add the pureed pumpkin with a pinch of salt, the thyme, onion and the crushed garlic
3. Allow the soup to boil then reduce the heat
4. Simmer for 30 minutes, it's not necessary to cover the pan
5. Transfer the soup to a blender and blend for 2-3 minutes, until it's smooth
6. Put the soup back in the pan and allow it to boil again, stirring continuously
7. Simmer for another 30 minutes, again uncovered
8. Add the heavy cream while stirring
9. Put the soup into bowls and sprinkle with parsley to finish

Czech Christmas Soup

SERVES 6
PREP TIME: 30 MINUTES | TOTAL: 90 MINUTES
NET CARBS: 47G | PROTEIN: 5G | FIBRE: 3G | FAT: 21G
KCAL:284

Ingredients
- 400g fresh peas – defrosted frozen ones will do
- 1 carrot, topped and tailed then cut into chunks
- 1 onion, remove the skin and cut it into quarters
- 2 pieces of celery cut into large chunks
- 3 cloves of garlic, peeled and crushed
- 1 litre vegetable stock
- Herbs as desired

Instructions
1. Find a good-sized pan and add the peas, celery, carrot, onion, and garlic
2. Mix then keep stirring as you add the vegetable stock
3. Put the pan on the stove on high heat
4. Stir continuously as it comes to the boil
5. Reduce the heat and allow it to simmer for 1 hour. You should keep the pan covered and stir occasionally during this
6. Transfer the soup to a blender and blend until smooth
7. Put it back into the pan and bring it back to the boil, allowing it to simmer for another 10-15 minutes
8. Serve with your choice of garnish

Nutty Pumpkin Delight

SERVES 4
PREP TIME: 15 MINUTES | TOTAL: 35 MINUTES
NET CARBS: 23G | PROTEIN: 13G | FIBRE: 7G | FAT: 30G
KCAL:576

Ingredients
- 2 tbsp olive oil
- 1 onion, peeled and chopped
- 2 cloves of garlic, peeled and crushed
- 1600ml chicken stock
- 1 pumpkin, deseeded with innards pureed
- 1 tbsp brown sugar
- 200ml whipping cream
- 200g pecans, chopped into small pieces and toasted
- Pinch thyme, cumin, and rosemary
- Salt and pepper to taste

Instructions
1. Place a large pan on your hob and turn it on to high heat
2. Add the olive oil and chopped onion, and sauté for 3 minutes to soften
3. Put the garlic in and cook for another minute
4. Now add the chicken stock; pureed pumpkin, brown sugar and herbs
5. Stir continuously and allow the mixture to start boiling then reduce the heat
6. Let the soup simmer for 10 minutes, it will thicken
7. Add the cream and pecans and cook for another 1-2 minutes
8. Remove from the heat and transfer to your blender. Blend for as long as necessary to make the soup smooth
9. Put the soup back into the pan and reheat, once hot it's ready to serve

Curried Acorn Soup

SERVES 6
PREP TIME: 50 MINUTES | TOTAL: 1HR 10 MINUTES
NET CARBS: 31G | PROTEIN: 13G | FIBRE: 8G | FAT: 12G
KCAL:228

Ingredients
- 3 acorn squash, cut them in half and remove all the seeds
- 1 onion, peeled and finely chopped
- 2 tbsp olive oil
- 600ml chicken stock
- 300ml cream
- 2 tbsp curry powder
- Pinch of nutmeg
- Salt and pepper if desired

Instructions
1. Turn the oven on and preheat to 175°C
2. Lightly grease a tray then put your acorn squash halves on a tray, face down
3. Put the tray in the oven and cook the squash for 35-40 minutes
4. Separately, put a pan on the hob set to medium heat
5. Ladd the oil, onion, and curry powder
6. Cook for 3-5 minutes until the onion is soft, take it off the hob
7. Remove the acorn squash from the oven and scoop the squash out of the shell
8. Put the squash pulp in with the onion and with the chicken stock and stir as you gradually bring it to the boil
9. Simmer for 20 minutes
10. Move the soup to your blender and blend until smooth
11. Put the soup back in the pan and place it on the hob over a medium heat
12. Stir continuously while adding the cream and nutmeg
13. Taste and add salt and pepper if required
14. Serve with the garnish of your choice

Butternut & Garlic Soup (works against vampires)

SERVES 6
PREP TIME: 15 MINUTES | TOTAL: 40 MINUTES
NET CARBS: 21G | PROTEIN: 12G | FIBRE: 3G | FAT: 28G
KCAL: 388

Ingredients
- 2 tbsp olive oil
- 1 onion, peeled and finely sliced
- 8 cloves of garlic, peeled and roughly chopped
- 800ml vegetable stock
- 2 butternut squash, peeled and cut into cubes
- 400ml cream
- 8 strips of bacon – you'll need to cook them under the grill and cut them into small pieces
- 1 tsp ground cinnamon
- Pinch of nutmeg
- 200g cheddar cheese, crumble it in your hands

Instructions
1. Put the oil in a pan over the hob on a medium heat
2. Once the oil is warm add the onion and garlic
3. Allow them to cook for 4-5 minutes, tossing frequently
4. Drop in the cinnamon and nutmeg and cook for another minute
5. Now slowly add the stock and the butternut squash cubes
6. Allow the soup to come to the boil then reduce the heat
7. Cover the pan and leave to simmer for 20 minutes
8. Transfer to the blender and let it make the soup smooth for you
9. Move it back to the pan and, while reheating, add the cream
10. Taste and add salt and pepper if required
11. Drop in the pieces of bacon and stir for another minute
12. Remove from the heat, ladle into bowls and sprinkle the cheese on top

Spring Soup

SERVES 6
PREP TIME: 20 MINUTES | TOTAL: 45 MINUTES
NET CARBS: 21G | PROTEIN: 6G | FIBRE: 3G | FAT: 5G
KCAL:147

Ingredients
- 1 tbsp olive oil
- 1 carrot, topped and tailed then finely sliced
- 1 red pepper, deseeded and sliced
- 1 leek cut into long strips
- 1 litre vegetable stock
- 2 crushed garlic cloves
- 2 potatoes, peeled then cut into small chunks
- 6 pieces of asparagus – cut into small sections
- 1 tsp sugar
- Salt and pepper to taste

Instructions
1. Place your pan on the hob on a medium heat
2. Add the olive oil and warm before adding leek, red pepper, and carrot
3. Sauté for 5 minutes until tender
4. Add the garlic and cook for another minute
5. Slowly stir in the stock and chunks of potato while heating the soup
6. Bring it to the boil and let it simmer for 5-10 minutes
7. Put the asparagus, sugar, and any salt and pepper into the mix and simmer for another 5 minutes
8. Make sure the vegetables are tender
9. You can serve like this or blend it until smooth first, the choice is yours

Mulligatawny Soup

SERVES 4
PREP TIME: 15 MINUTES | TOTAL: 65 MINUTES
NET CARBS: 37G | PROTEIN: 12G | FIBRE: 8G | FAT: 12G
KCAL:321

Ingredients
- 2 tbsp olive oil
- 20g unsalted butter
- 1 onion, peeled and sliced
- 2 pieces of celery – cut into thin slices
- 3 carrots, topped and tailed, then chopped into chunks
- 1 parsnip, topped and tailed, then chopped into chunks
- 2 crushed cloves of garlic
- Piece of root ginger, peeled then grated
- 1 apple, peeled and cut into small pieces
- 2 tbsp curry powder
- 1 tsp ground cumin
- 2 litres of chicken stock
- 1 tbsp tomato puree
- 100g rice – your choice of which type, basmati is a good choice
- 1 tbsp lemon, juice

Instructions
1. Place the butter and oil in your pan over medium heat and warm
2. Once the butter has melted add the onion and celery
3. Cook for 10 minutes to soften
4. Add the carrots, ginger, apple, and crushed garlic then cook for another 1-2 minutes
5. Now introduce the tomato puree, curry powder and cumin, stirring continuously
6. Slowly pour in the stock and bring to the boil
7. Cover and allow to simmer for 40 minutes
8. While the soup is simmering cook your rice according to the instructions on the packet
9. Once cooked, drain and rinse the rice before stirring it into the soup with the lemon juice
10. Serve immediately

Turkey Noodle Soup

SERVES 4
PREP TIME: 10 MINUTES | TOTAL: 20 MINUTES
NET CARBS: 36G | PROTEIN: 23G | FIBRE: 5G | FAT: 6G
KCAL:285

Ingredients
- 140g egg noodles
- 200g cooked turkey – Christmas leftovers are perfect
- 1.2 litres of chicken stock
- 4 carrots, washed, topped and tailed, then sliced
- 200g peas – fresh or frozen
- 1 onion, peeled and finely sliced

Instructions
1. Put the stock in a pan over high heat and bring it to the boil
2. Allow the stock to boil for 4-5 minutes
3. Reduce the heat and add your egg noodles
4. Let them simmer for 3-5 minutes until soft
5. Add your turkey, onions, and peas
6. Continue cooking while stirring for 2-3 minutes, make sure the soup is hot right the way through
7. Dish into bowls and serve

CREAMY SOUPS

Ham & Potato Soup

SERVES 8
PREP TIME: 20 MINUTES | TOTAL: 40 MINUTES
NET CARBS: 20G | PROTEIN: 6G | FIBRE: 5G | FAT: 11G
KCAL: 195

Ingredients
- 4 potatoes, peeled then cut into small cubes
- 1 litre chicken stock
- 400g cooked ham, cut into small pieces
- 4 pieces celery finely sliced
- 2 onions, peeled then finely sliced
- 50g unsalted butter
- 100g flour
- 300ml milk – full or semi
- Salt and pepper to taste

Instructions
1. Put the ham, potatoes, celery, and chicken stock into a pan over a high heat
2. Stir continuously while bringing the mixture to the boil
3. Reduce the heat and simmer for 15 minutes
4. Add salt and pepper if required
5. Put your butter in a different pan and let it melt over a medium heat
6. Mix in the flour to the butter slowly, keeping it as a smooth paste
7. Add the milk, and keep stirring as you cook for another 5 minutes, it should thicken to a paste
8. Blend the milk mixture into the chicken stock and vegetables, stirring constantly while on medium heat
9. Once blended properly serve

Creamy Chicken & Wild Rice

SERVES 8
PREP TIME: 5 MINUTES | TOTAL: 35 MINUTES
NET CARBS: 23G | PROTEIN: 12G | FIBRE: 8G | FAT: 37G
KCAL:463

Ingredients
- 400g chicken breast, cook it and then tear it into small pieces
- 800ml chicken stock
- 400ml water
- 1 packet wild rice
- 200g flour
- 100g butter
- 300ml cream
- Salt and pepper to taste

Instructions
1. Put a large pan on the stove and turn it on to medium heat
2. Pour in the chicken stock and chicken
3. Bring the mixture to the boil then add your packet of wild rice
4. Take the pan off the heat
5. In a separate pan over medium heat put the butter and allow it to melt
6. Add the flour slowly, whisking as you do to ensure it's smooth
7. Add salt and pepper if desired
8. Now add the cream while whisking to ensure the sauce is smooth and fully integrated
9. Return the stock pan to the heat and slowly add the flour mixture to it
10. Once fully blended, make sure it's on low heat
11. Cover, and simmer for 15 minutes
12. Serve and enjoy

Creamy Tomato Basil Soup

SERVES 4
PREP TIME: 10 MINUTES | TOTAL: 45 MINUTES
NET CARBS: 17G | PROTEIN: 4G | FIBRE: 3G | FAT: 45G
KCAL:473

Ingredients
- 6 large tomatoes, remove the skin and the seeds before dicing them
- 800ml tomato juice
- 200 ml cream
- 50g butter
- Fresh basil leaves
- Salt and pepper if desired

Instructions
1. Start by putting the tomatoes and tomato juice in a large pan
2. Put the pan on the hob over medium heat and bring the mixture to the boil
3. Reduce heat and simmer for 30 minutes
4. Take the pot off the stove and add your basil leaves
5. Transfer to a blender and blend until smooth. If you prefer you can use a hand blender in the pan
6. Add the cream and butter
7. Return the pan to the hob on medium heat and keep stirring
8. Don't let it boil as the butter melts and the ingredients combine
9. Taste and add salt and pepper if desired

Creamy Potato & Leek Soup

SERVES 6
PREP TIME: 20 MINUTES | TOTAL: 60 MINUTES
NET CARBS: 58G | PROTEIN: 17G | FIBRE: 7G | FAT: 50G
KCAL:739

Ingredients
- 8 potatoes, peeled then cut into small squares
- 800ml chicken stock
- 1 tbsp olive oil
- 400g bacon, you'll need to cut it into small pieces
- 4 leeks, finely sliced
- 300ml cream

Instructions
1. Put your pan on, the stove on medium heat and add the chicken stock
2. Bring it to the boil then add the potatoes squares
3. Simmer for 10-15 minutes until the potatoes are soft
4. In a separate pan put your olive oil and heat on a low heat
5. Once warm add the bacon pieces and sauté for 5-10 minutes until browned
6. Remove the bacon and place it on a kitchen towel to absorb extra grease
7. Add the leeks to the pan and sauté for another 10 minutes
8. Now slowly stir the bacon, leeks, and cream into the chicken stock
9. Keep heating for 5 minutes until fully blended and thickened
10. Serve and eat hot

Chicken Gnocchi Soup

SERVES 4
PREP TIME: 10 MINUTES | TOTAL: 25 MINUTES
NET CARBS: 57G | PROTEIN: 36G | FIBRE: 5G | FAT: 34G
KCAL:671

Ingredients
- 1 tbsp olive oil
- 10g unsalted butter
- 1 small onion, peeled then cut into small pieces
- 2 pieces celery, finely sliced
- 4 carrots, topped and tailed then grated
- 3 crushed cloves of garlic
- 25g flour
- 800ml chicken stock
- 600g cooked chicken, cut into small pieces
- Salt and pepper to taste
- 400g potato gnocchi
- 200g spinach, finely chopped
- 250ml cream
- Little parmesan cheese

Instructions
1. Pick a large pan and put it on the hob over a medium heat
2. Add your butter and oil and warm until the butter has melted
3. Drop in the celery, carrots, crushed garlic, and onion
4. Add salt and pepper if desired and cook for 3-4 minutes, the onions should be transparent
5. Now slowly add the flour and continue to sauté
6. Pour in the chicken stock, stirring continuously as you do so
7. Drop in the cooked chicken pieces and potato gnocchi
8. Continue cooking on medium heat for another 3-4 minutes, making sure the chicken is warm
9. Lower the heat and slowly add the cream, stirring as you do so
10. Add the spinach and any salt and pepper if desired
11. Serve by itself or with fresh bread

Creamy Tortellini Soup

SERVES 4
PREP TIME: 5 MINUTES | TOTAL: 15 MINUTES
NET CARBS: 32G | PROTEIN: 16G | FIBRE: 5G | FAT: 34G
KCAL:258

Ingredients
- 1.2 litres of vegetable broth
- 200ml cream
- 500g frozen peas and carrots – you can also use fresh thinly sliced if you prefer
- 400g fresh tortellini pasta
- Salt and pepper to taste
- A little olive oil
- Parmesan cheese

Instructions
1. Put your pan on the hob and turn it to medium
2. Add the vegetable stock and slowly bring it to the boil, stirring occasionally
3. Now add the peas and carrots and bring the pan back to the boil
4. Drop in the pasta and simmer the mixture for 5-10 minutes, until the tortellini is soft
5. Add your cream and, as you stir it in, keep cooking for another 2-3 minutes
6. Taste and adjust with salt and pepper if required
7. Dish into bowls and garnish with the parmesan cheese then drizzle a little olive oil across the top

Cordon Bleu Soup

SERVES 4
PREP TIME: 10 MINUTES | TOTAL: 30 MINUTES
NET CARBS: 42G | PROTEIN: 15G | FIBRE: 8G | FAT: 21G
KCAL:387

Ingredients

- 75g butter
- 1 onion, peeled and cut into small pieces
- 100g flour
- 600ml milk – full-fat or semi
- 250ml cream
- 400ml chicken stock
- 400g cooked chicken cut into small pieces
- 200g cooked ham, also cut into small pieces
- 1 tbsp mustard
- 200g cheddar cheese, grated
- 100g chopped parsley, finely diced
- Salt and pepper if desired

Instructions

1. Put the butter in a pan over medium heat and allow it to melt
2. Drop the onion pieces in the pan and cook for 10 minutes, allowing them to soften. Don't let them burn
3. Slowly add the flour and whisk the mixture to ensure it forms a smooth paste
4. Add half of the milk and half the cream to the mixture, stirring continuously
5. Bring the mixture to the boil and slowly add the rest of the milk and cream
6. Allow the mixture to simmer for 2-3 minutes
7. Now add your cooked chicken and ham, the mustard, cheese, and parsley
8. Make sure the cheese is melted before lifting the pan off the heat and serving

Creamy Mushroom

SERVES 8
PREP TIME: 5 MINUTES | TOTAL: 45 MINUTES
NET CARBS: 35G | PROTEIN: 17G | FIBRE: 9G | FAT: 18G
KCAL: 361

Ingredients
- 4 tbsp olive oil
- 600g button mushrooms, finely sliced
- 1 onion, peeled and finely sliced
- 2 pieces celery, cut into thin strips
- 4 crushed cloves of garlic
- 75g flour
- 1 glass of white wine
- 800ml vegetable stock
- 250ml cream
- 1 tbsp balsamic vinegar
- Pinch of ground parsley and thyme
- Salt and pepper to taste

Instructions
1. Place a pan on the stove over medium heat and add the olive oil
2. Once warm put the mushrooms in the pan and cook for 5-7 minutes until they are a golden brown
3. Now add the onion, celery, and thyme and cook for another 5 minutes
4. Drop the flour into the pan and keep stirring as you cook for a further minute
5. Keep the pan on the heat as you add the wine and any salt and pepper you desire
6. As it starts to boil add the stock, and stir continuously to ensure there are no lumps
7. Once it starts to boil, reduce the heat and let it simmer for 20 minutes
8. Take it off the stove and let it cool before blending the mixture until smooth
9. Now put it back in the pan and reheat while stirring in the cream and balsamic vinegar
10. Serve and enjoy

Creamy Carrot Soup

SERVES 6
PREP TIME: 20 MINUTES | TOTAL: 50 MINUTES
NET CARBS: 23G | PROTEIN: 8G | FIBRE: 8G | FAT: 22G
KCAL:346

Ingredients
- 8 carrots, topped and tailed then sliced
- 400ml chicken stock
- 2 crushed garlic cloves
- Zest from one lemon
- 400ml cream
- Pinch of nutmeg
- Salt and pepper to taste
- Fresh herbs as desired

Instructions
1. Take a pan and put on medium heat
2. Pour in the chicken stock and add the crushed garlic with lemon zest, along with your carrots
3. Bring to the boil, reduce the heat, and simmer for 20 minutes
4. Remove from the heat and allow to cool slightly before transferring to a blender
5. Blend until smooth
6. Return to the pan and slowly stir in the cream along with the nutmeg and any salt and pepper you feel it needs
7. Reheat the soup for 3-5 minutes and then serve
8. Garnish with the herbs of your choice

Beer Cheese Soup

SERVES 6
PREP TIME: 15 MINUTES | TOTAL: 40 MINUTES
NET CARBS: 10G | PROTEIN: 20G | FIBRE: 1G | FAT: 43G
KCAL:618

Ingredients

- 400g bacon, cut into small pieces
- 1 onion, peeled and diced
- 1 red pepper, deseeded and finely sliced
- 1 jalapeno, deseeded and finely sliced
- 100g flour
- 100g butter
- 800ml chicken stock
- 500ml beer of your choice
- 250ml cream
- 600g cheddar cheese, grated
- Salt and pepper if desired

Instructions

1. Start by using a drop of oil to cook the bacon pieces, it should take 5-7 minutes to get them crispy
2. Remove the bacon from the pan and place it on some kitchen towel to absorb excess grease
3. Place the onion, pepper, jalapeno and any herbs you like in the pan with the butter
4. Keep the heat low and cook until the vegetables are soft and tender, roughly 5 minutes
5. Add the flour, stirring to ensure it is fully integrated
6. Pour your beer in slowly, mixing as you do so. It will start to thicken
7. Now add your chicken stock while stirring continuously
8. Drop in the cheese and the bacon and cook for another 3-5 minutes while stirring
9. Ladle into the bowls and serve with a garnish of chives

Irish Parsnip Soup

SERVES 4
PREP TIME: 15 MINUTES | TOTAL: 45 MINUTES
NET CARBS: 28G | PROTEIN: 9G | FIBRE: 2G | FAT: 12G
KCAL:187

Ingredients

- 4 parsnips, they'll need to be peeled and then cut into chunks
- 4 pieces of celery finely sliced
- 2 onions, peeled and finely sliced
- 2 crushed garlic cloves
- 300ml vegetable stock
- 100ml cream
- 2 tbsp olive oil
- 1 tbsp white miso sauce
- Salt and pepper if desired

Instructions

1. Put your olive oil into the pan and place it on the hob over a medium heat
2. Once warm, add the garlic, celery, and onion and simmer for 5 minutes until they've softened
3. Drop the parsnip chunks into the pan and let it cook for another 5 minutes
4. Now add your vegetable stock, bring the mixture to the boil, and simmer for 20 minutes
5. Slowly stir in the cream, white miso, and any salt/pepper you want
6. Transfer the soup to a blender and blend until smooth. If you prefer you can use a hand blender in the pan
7. Reheat as necessary to ensure it is piping hot before serving

VEGAN SOUPS

Tomato, Chickpea & Pasta Soup

SERVES 2
PREP TIME: 20 MINUTES | TOTAL: 50 MINUTES
NET CARBS: 36G | PROTEIN: 14G | FIBRE: 10G | FAT: 15G
KCAL: 391

Ingredients
- 2 cloves of garlic – finely chopped
- 1 tin chickpeas (400g)
- 1 tin chopped tomatoes (also 400g)
- 400ml vegetable stock
- 1 Tbsp olive oil
- 50g pasta – your choice of which type

Instructions
1. Start by putting the olive oil into a pan on the stove and heating gently.
2. Once warm, add the garlic and cook until brown, stirring regularly
3. Add your chopped tomatoes and the pasta
4. Once fully blended pour in the vegetable stock, stirring continuously
5. Keep stirring as you bring the mixture to the boil
6. Reduce the heat and allow the soup to simmer for 15-20 minutes. The longer it simmers the softer the pasta will be
7. Add salt, pepper, or any other seasoning you like
8. Serve and enjoy, if you wish you can drizzle a little olive oil across the top. It adds flavour and looks great.

Vegan Noodle Soup

SERVES
PREP TIME: 20 MINUTES | TOTAL: 30 MINUTES
NET CARBS: 32G | PROTEIN: 12G | FIBRE: 10G | FAT: 12G
KCAL: 280

Ingredients
- 2 packets of noodle soup – any brand dried or tinned
- 300g wheat or rice noodles, making sure they are vegan friendly
- Small piece of root ginger – you'll need to finely grate this
- 200g broccoli – frozen or fresh. Cut into small pieces
- 4 spring onions
- 1 chilli pepper – optional, if you don't like the heat leave it out
- Pinch of sesame seeds
- 1 tbsp lime juice

Instructions
1. Take a pan and put your noodle soup in it. Tinned can be poured straight in, dried soup will need to be added to the right amount of water, it will say how much on the tin. It's best to use boiled water as it saves time and energy heating it on the stove
2. Bring the pan to the boil
3. Add your grated ginger and the wheat or rice noodles, and the lime juicer
4. Stir regularly as you bring the soup back to the boil and allow it to simmer for 2-3 minutes
5. Drop the broccoli pieces into the pan and let it simmer for another 5 minutes
6. Your soup should be ready. Taste it and add seasoning or salt and pepper if desired. This is optional
7. Ladle the soup into bowls and sprinkle the top with the finely chopped onion, sesame seeds, and the chilli – if you're using it
8. Enjoy! You'll be wanting to make it again

Roast Cauliflower, Cumin & Coconut Milk Soup

SERVES 4
PREP TIME: 15 MINUTES | TOTAL: 45 MINUTES
NET CARBS: 32G | PROTEIN: 13G | FIBRE: 8G | FAT: 8G
KCAL: 294

Ingredients
- 400g frozen cauliflower stalks or 1 large fresh cauliflower cut into small pieces
- 2 cloves of garlic – finely sliced
- 600ml of vegetable stock
- 400g tin of coconut milk
- Pinch cumin seeds
- 1 tbsp olive oil
- Pinch chilli flakes – if desired

Instructions
1. Unusually for a soup, you're going to need the oven for this one. Preheat to 190°c or 170°C if you have a fan-assisted one (that's gas mark 7)
2. Put your cauliflower and garlic pieces on a baking tray and drizzle them with olive oil
3. Sprinkle cumin seeds across the top of the cauliflower
4. Ass the chilli flakes if you want to use them. You can also cover the cauliflower and garlic with salt and pepper if desired
5. Finally, drizzle the olive oil across the cauliflower and onion and slide it into the oven for 25 minutes
6. While it's cooking, put your vegetable stock and coconut milk into a pan and slowly bring it to the boil on your stove. Stir constantly and reduce the temperature as soon as it reaches boiling
7. Remove the cauliflower and garlic from the oven and add them to your pan
8. Allow it to simmer for 10 minutes, stirring regularly
9. Take the pan off the heat and pour the contents into a blender
10. Blend for 1-2 minutes until it's smooth
11. Put it back into the pan to reheat if necessary, before serving with a garnish of your choice

Pumpkin, Chilli, & Coconut Soup

SERVES 4
PREP TIME: 20 MINUTES | TOTAL: 45 MINUTES
NET CARBS: 14G | PROTEIN: 3G | FIBRE: 3G | FAT: 11G
KCAL: 177

Ingredients
- 1 pumpkin – you'll need to cut this into small wedges or cubes
- 1 onion – peeled and finely chopped
- 2 cloves of garlic – also chopped into small pieces
- 1 small piece of root ginger – finely grated
- Pinch red chilli flakes, if desired
- 400ml coconut milk (1 tin)
- Thyme or other herbs to season

Instructions
1. You'll need a large pan, the larger your pumpkin the bigger the pan
2. Place all the pumpkin in the pan and add the onion, garlic, and chilli if you're using it
3. Add approximately 400-500ml of water, it's better to add less and increase it than to add too much at the start
4. Put the pan on the stove on medium heat and bring the mixture to the boil
5. It should take 10-15 minutes to reduce the pumpkin to a pulp
6. Now add the coconut milk and continue simmering for 5-10 minutes
7. Taste the soup and add salt, pepper, and any herbs you desire
8. Serve hot and enjoy

Carrot & Ginger Soup

SERVES 1
PREP TIME: 20 MINUTES | TOTAL: 40 MINUTES
NET CARBS: 12G | PROTEIN: 2G | FIBRE: 10G | FAT: 5G
KCAL:160

Ingredients
- 1 clove garlic chopped into small pieces
- 1 onion peeled and finely sliced
- 350ml vegetable stock
- 1200g carrots – top and tailed then cut into small circular pieces
- 1 tsp rapeseed or olive oil
- 1 medium piece of ginger root – peeled and cut into small pieces
- Spring onion for serving, if desired

Instructions
1. Put the rapeseed or olive oil into a pan and place on the stove over a medium heat
2. Once the oil has warmed, slide the onion into the pan and let it simmer for 3 minutes
3. Then, add the carrots, ginger, and garlic. Keep stirring as you allow the pan to simmer for 5 minutes
4. Pour in the stock and bring the mixture to the boil
5. Simmer for approximately 20 minutes to ensure the carrots are soft
6. Taste and add salt, pepper, or any other spice to create your desired taste
7. Put the mixture into a blender and blend until smooth, that should be 2-3 minutes
8. Reheat on the stove and, once warm, serve with any desired garnish

Carrot & Coriander delight

SERVES 4
PREP TIME: 15 MINUTES | TOTAL: 30 MINUTES
NET CARBS: 12G | PROTEIN: 2G | FIBRE: 4G | FAT: 4G
KCAL:87

Ingredients
- 500g carrots, preferably fresh which are top and tailed, peeled, and then sliced into long pieces. If not, frozen carrots will do
- 1 onion – cut into small pieces
- 1.2 litres of vegetable stock
- Large pinch ground coriander
- 1 tbsp olive oil or the oil of your choice
- Salt & pepper to taste

Instructions
1. Start by heating the oil in a pan on your hob. Do this over a medium heat
2. Once the oil is warm add your carrot pieces and onion, and allow to simmer for 4 minutes, this should soften the carrots
3. Add your ground coriander, stirring continuously to blend
4. Taste while simmering the mixture for another minute, you can add salt and pepper if desired
5. Pour in all the vegetable stock and bring the pan back to the boil
6. Simmer the soup for another 12-15 minutes, ensuring all the vegetables are tender
7. Transfer the soup to a blender and blend for 1-2 minutes until smooth
8. Return it to your pan and reheat before serving
9. Adding a pinch of coriander to each bowl creates an artistic flair

Sweet Potato Soup

SERVES 4
PREP TIME: 20 MINUTES | TOTAL: 40 MINUTES
NET CARBS: 27G | PROTEIN: 3G | FIBRE: 9G | FAT: 4G
KCAL: 234

Ingredients

- 1 large onion chopped into medium-sized pieces
- 2 carrots, topped and tailed then sliced into long lengths
- 1700g sweet potatoes – washed, peeled, then cubed
- 1.2 litres of vegetable stock
- 1 tbsp olive oil – or a similar oil of your choice
- Small piece of ginger root, chopped into small pieces or grated
- Pinch red chilli flakes, if desired
- Clove of garlic crushed

Instructions

1. Place a pan on the hob and put the olive oil into it. You'll find it's best to use a lid as you gently warm the oil
2. Tip the onion and chopped carrots into the pan, replace the lid and allow to simmer for 4-5 minutes, this will soften the vegetables
3. Add the garlic, ginger, and chilli, if you're using it
4. Stir while keeping the pan on the heat for 2-3 minutes
5. Mix in the sweet potato and then slowly add the vegetable stock while stirring
6. Cover and simmer again for 15 minutes
7. To fully enjoy the soup, you'll want to transfer it to a blender and blend for 2-3 minutes until it's smooth
8. Reheat if necessary, before dishing it into bowls and serving

Bean & Vegan Pesto Soup

SERVES 4
PREP TIME: 15 MINUTES | TOTAL: 45 MINUTES
NET CARBS: 27G | PROTEIN: 13G | FIBRE: 12G | FAT: 24G
KCAL:402

Ingredients
- 1 onion, peeled and finely chopped
- 2 sticks of celery – washed and also finely sliced
- 1 courgette – cut into small pieces
- 2 carrots – also cut into small pieces
- 2 tbsp olive oil or the oil of your choice
- 2 cloves of garlic – crushed
- 400g tin of French beans
- 400g tin of white beans, also known as haricot blanc
- 1 litre vegetable stock
- 1 small jar of pesto

Instructions
1. It should be noted that you can make your own pesto but it is simpler to purchase a jar, just make sure it's vegan-friendly
2. Place the oil in a saucepan and heat on the hob
3. Once warm, add your celery, courgette, onion, and carrots
4. Cover the pan and allow the mixture to simmer for 10 minutes, it softens the vegetables
5. Add your crushed garlic and stir while heating for another minute
6. You can now add both tins of beans to your mixture and the vegetable stock
7. Keep stirring as you bring it to the boil and then, turn the heat down, allowing it to simmer
8. As it simmers stir in your jar of pesto
9. Let the soup simmer for five minutes and then serve

Butternut Squash Soup

SERVES 8
PREP TIME: 30 MINUTES | TOTAL: 110 MINUTES
NET CARBS: 29G | PROTEIN: 9G | FIBRE: 4G | FAT: 5G
KCAL:198

Ingredients

- It should be noted you'll need a large saucepan when making this quantity of soup. If preferred, you can half the ingredients
- 21.5kg butternut squash – this is after peeling and deseeding the squash. It also needs to be cut into small cubes
- 2 carrots, topped and tailed, peeled, and chopped into small pieces
- 1 onion – peel it then cut it into small pieces
- 1 pepper – preferably red finely sliced
- 4 tbsp olive oil or the oil of your choice
- Small piece of root ginger, washed, peeled, and grated
- 1.5 litres of vegetable stock
- 1 tablespoon of honey to sweeten, if desired

Instructions

1. Turn your oven on and set it to 200°c, or 180°c if its fan-assisted (gas mark 6)
2. Start by putting your butternut squash, already chopped, into a freezer bag. It should be resealable
3. Add the onion pieces, carrots, and red pepper, along with 2 tbsp of olive oil and salt/pepper if desired
4. Seal the bag and give it a good shake to mix
5. Pour the contents onto your roasting tray and slide them into the oven for 40 minutes
6. If you want to sweeten add the honey by drizzling it across the vegetables after 35 minutes then continue to cook them
7. Separately, put your large pan on the hob and warm the rest of the oil
8. Once it reaches temperature add your ginger and heat for approximately one minute
9. Add your vegetable stock and bring it to the boil
10. Tip in your vegetables and allow the soup to simmer for a few minutes
11. Transfer the contents to your blender, which may take several loads, and blend until smooth
12. Reheat before serving with your chosen accompaniment

Spicy Mexican Bean Soup

SERVES 6
PREP TIME: 20 MINUTES | TOTAL: 40 MINUTES
NET CARBS: 13G | PROTEIN: 5G | FIBRE: 6G | FAT: 1G
KCAL:94

Ingredients
- 1 onion chopped into small pieces
- 2 garlic cloves crushed
- 2 carrots – topped and tailed, then peeled and cut into small pieces
- 1 pepper – preferably red, finely sliced
- 1 vegetable stock cube
- 400g tin of red kidney beans
- Pinch chilli powder, if desired
- 1 tsp olive oil
- Pinch ground cumin
- 400g tin of chopped tomatoes
- Pinch dried oregano

Instructions
1. Put your garlic, onion, and carrots into a microwaveable bowl and mix them thoroughly together
2. Put the bowl in the microwave on high for 3 minutes
3. Place 400ml of boiling water, from the kettle will do, in a jug with the vegetable stock cube and mix until it is fully dissolved
4. Empty the tin of kidney beans into a colander, rinse them with tap water, and allow them to drain
5. Put your oregano, cumin, pepper, chilli powder, and oil in the bowl with the garlic and carrots
6. Mix and cook in the microwave for another minute
7. Now add the chopped tomatoes and microwave again, this time for 15 minutes on full power
8. Check the flavour and add salt and pepper if desired
9. Transfer it to a blender to make the soup smooth
10. Put it back in the microwaveable bowl and add the kidney beans
11. Cook on full power for another 3 minutes before serving

Lemongrass & Peppercorn Soup

SERVES 4
PREP TIME: 20 MINUTES | TOTAL: 50 MINUTES
NET CARBS: 39G | PROTEIN: 9G | FIBRE: 4G | FAT: 46G
KCAL:612

Ingredients
- 4 tbsp coconut oil
- 2 cloves of garlic
- 1 green chilli – remove the stems
- 4 spring onions – chop them
- Small piece of fresh ginger, peeled and chopped into pieces
- Large pinch turmeric
- 800ml coconut milk
- 3 tbsp lime juice
- 400ml vegetable stock
- 1 tbsp soy sauce
- 1 lemongrass stalk
- Small butternut squash, peeled, deseeded, and sliced
- 100g fresh spinach – finely chopped
- 100g rice noodles

Instructions
1. The first job is to warm your coconut oil in a pan
2. While it's melting blend the garlic, ginger, and chillies with your spring onions
3. Add the melted coconut oil and blend again
4. Put the mixture back into the pan and warm
5. Now slowly add the turmeric and coconut milk along with half the lime juice, the soy sauce, and the vegetable stock
6. Add your lemon grass, smashed but still in one piece, and the butternut squash, and simmer for 5-10 minutes
7. Separately put your noodles in a bowl and cover them with boiling water from the kettle
8. Now add the spinach to the mixture and continue simmering while you drain the noodles
9. Mix the noodles with the soup and heat for another 1-2 minutes before serving

German Potato Soup

SERVES 4
PREP TIME: 15 MINUTES | TOTAL: 40 MINUTES
NET CARBS: 43G | PROTEIN: 5G | FIBRE: 8G | FAT: 6G
KCAL: 265

Ingredients
- 1 tbsp olive oil
- 1 onion, peeled and finely sliced
- 3 cloves of garlic crushed
- 2 pieces of celery cut into small pieces
- 2 carrots, cut into small pieces
- 1900g potatoes – peeled and cut into cubes
- Pinch of nutmeg
- 1 litre of vegetable broth
- Small tin coconut milk
- Fresh parsley chopped

Instructions
1. Heat your oil first in a pan over the stove and add the onion. Let it simmer for 2-3 minutes until it starts to brown
2. Add the carrots, celery, garlic, and potato pieces
3. Keep simmering for another minute
4. Add your vegetable broth and bring the mixture to the boil, it's faster if you use boiling water to make the vegetable broth
5. Leave it to simmer for 20 minutes
6. Transfer the soup to a blender and blend for several minutes until it's smooth. You may need to split the soup
7. Return it to the pan and add the coconut milk, allowing the mixture to continue simmering for another 2—3 minutes
8. Add salt, pepper, or any other flavourings you wish before serving

GLUTEN-FREE SOUPS

Minestrone Soup

SERVES 6
PREP TIME: 10 MINUTES | TOTAL: 50 MINUTES
NET CARBS: 48G | PROTEIN: 16G | FIBRE: 12G | FAT: 9G
KCAL:329

Ingredients
- 1 onion sliced into small pieces
- 3 carrots topped, tailed, peeled, and cut into small sections
- 2 pieces of celery finely sliced
- 3 cloves of garlic crushed
- 2 tbsp olive oil
- 2 tbsp tomato puree
- Small tin chopped tomatoes
- 1 litre vegetable stock
- Italian season – if desired
- Small tin red kidney beans, drained and rinsed with cold water
- Small tin chick peas, also drained and rinsed with cold water
- Small cabbage cut into small pieces

Instructions
1. You can make this in a pan but it is easier in a Dutch oven
2. Melt the olive oil in your pan and add the onion, celery, and carrots
3. Let it simmer for 10 minutes
4. Put the crushed garlic and tomato puree in the pan and heat for another minute
5. Place everything else into the pan and bring the mixture to the boil
6. Turn the heat down and allow it to simmer for 25 minutes, stirring occasionally
7. Remove from the heat, add any additional seasonings you desire, and serve
8. It improves the flavour to sprinkle parmesan cheese on the top when serving, it's naturally gluten-free

Carrot & White Bean

SERVES 4
PREP TIME: 10 MINUTES | TOTAL: 35 MINUTES
NET CARBS: 46G | PROTEIN: 14G | FIBRE: 9G | FAT: 11G
KCAL: 345

Ingredients
- 1 tbsp olive oil
- 1 onion, peeled and finely chopped
- Small piece of fresh ginger, peeled and cut into small pieces
- 4 cloves of garlic crushed
- 400g carrots, topped, tailed, and chopped into small pieces
- 400g tin, of white beans – drain the tin and rinse the beans in fresh cold water
- Salt and pepper to taste
- 500ml vegetable stock

Instructions
1. Put your olive oil into a saucepan and heat it over the stove
2. Once warm, add the onion and cook them for 2-3 minutes, they'll go translucent
3. Add your garlic and ginger and simmer for another 3-5 minutes, stirring continuously
4. Pour in the carrots, white beans, and your vegetable stock and bring the mixture to the boil
5. Reduce the heat and allow the soup to simmer for 20-25 minutes
6. Once the vegetables are tender, pour the contents into your blender and blend for several minutes, until smooth
7. Once smooth you can serve or reheat before serving if necessary

Keto Egg Soup

SERVES 2
PREP TIME: 5 MINUTES | TOTAL: 15 MINUTES
NET CARBS: 22G | PROTEIN: 9G | FIBRE: 3G | FAT: 21G
KCAL:1021

Ingredients
- 1 onion, peeled and finely sliced
- 1 tbsp butter – most kinds of butter are gluten-free but check
- 400ml organic chicken stock
- 1 tsp sesame oil or olive oil if you prefer
- Large pinch of ground coconut
- 4 eggs – beaten in a separate glass
- 2 spring onions washed and sliced, use only the green and white parts

Instructions
1. Start by putting a pan on the hob and turning the heat on
2. Add your butter and allow it to melt before sliding the onion in
3. Cook the onion for roughly 5 minutes to soften it without browning it
4. Now add your organic chicken stock and the ground coconut. Stir before adding your sesame or olive oil and, after tasting, any salt and pepper you desire
5. Bring the mixture back to the boil before turning the heat down
6. Allow the soup to simmer as you add the beaten eggs, you'll need to keep stirring while doing this
7. Simmer for at least five minutes before transferring to bowls and serving
8. You can sprinkle the spring onion pieces on top of the soup

Slow-Cooked Chicken Fajita Soup

SERVES 6
PREP TIME: 10 MINUTES | TOTAL: 4HR 10 MINUTES
NET CARBS: 42G | PROTEIN: 16G | FIBRE: 5G | FAT: 10G
KCAL:250

Ingredients
- 2 large tins of condensed cauliflower soup – check if it's gluten-free
- 1 standard jar of salsa
- 2 tsp chilli powder
- Pinch of ground cumin
- 3 peppers, deseeded and chopped into small pieces
- 3 onions, peeled and finely diced
- 500g chicken breast – cut into thin slices
- 2 tbsp lime juice

Instructions
1. You can use a slow cooker or a Dutch oven, the results are the same. It takes longer to cut the ingredients than it does to mix them
2. Simply add all your ingredients to the slow cooker
3. Cover the cooker and turn it on. You can choose a low setting and it will take approximately 8 hours to cook. Set the slow cooker on high and it should be done in 4 hours
4. Taste test when cooked in case you want to add salt, pepper, or any other seasoning
5. Once cooked simply serve, it couldn't be easier to get a delicious gluten-free soup

Asparagus & Spinach Soup

SERVES 4
PREP TIME: 15 MINUTES | TOTAL: 30 MINUTES
NET CARBS: 27G | PROTEIN: 12G | FIBRE: 6G | FAT: 9G
KCAL:186

Ingredients
- 2 tbsp olive oil – you can use coconut oil if you prefer
- 1 onion, peeled and finely chopped
- 200g fresh peas, it is possible to use frozen if fresh aren't available
- 2 tbsp coconut cream – this is optional
- 1 crushed garlic clove
- 600g fresh asparagus cut into small slices
- 1 piece fresh ginger root, washed, peeled, and grated
- 200g fresh spinach
- 600ml vegetable broth

Instructions
1. Choose your pan and place it on the hob. Add the olive or coconut oil and turn on the heat
2. Once the oil has melted slide in the onion, garlic, ginger, and asparagus
3. Simmer for 5 minutes, stirring regularly
4. Now chop the spinach and add it to the soup along with the vegetable broth
5. Bring the mixture back to the boil and simmer for 15 minutes
6. Put the soup into your blender and blend for several minutes until smooth
7. Return to the pan and reheat before serving
8. Add a swirl of coconut cream, a handful of fresh peas, (or frozen ones boiled for several minutes), and any salt and pepper that's needed

Sweet & Spicy Carrot Soup

SERVES 6
PREP TIME: MINUTES | TOTAL: MINUTES
NET CARBS: 43G | PROTEIN: 21G | FIBRE: 12G | FAT: 18G
KCAL:324

Ingredients
- 1 tbsp olive or coconut oil
- 1 small onion, peeled and finely sliced
- 6 carrots, topped, tailed, and sliced
- A large piece of fresh ginger, peeled and roughly chopped
- 2 tsp chilli flakes – if desired
- 800ml chicken stock
- 200ml coconut milk
- 1 tbsp brown sugar
- 1 tbsp lime juice

Instructions
1. The first step, as always, is to put your pan on the hob and turn on the heat
2. Add your olive or coconut oil and allow it to melt
3. Put the onions in the pan and simmer for 3-4 minutes, don't let them brown
4. Now add the ginger, carrot, and chilli, (if using)
5. Simmer for another 2-3 minutes
6. Add your chicken stock and simmer for roughly 30 minutes, allowing the carrots to become soft
7. Next, merge the mixture with the coconut milk, brown sugar, and the lime juice
8. Keep simmering for a couple of minutes before transferring it to your blender
9. Blend until smooth and then return the soup to the pan to reheat
10. Once warmed thoroughly, serve

Bean beef Soup

SERVES 4
PREP TIME: 15 MINUTES | TOTAL: 45 MINUTES
NET CARBS: 39G | PROTEIN: 19G | FIBRE: 12G | FAT: 21G
KCAL:352

Ingredients

- 1 tbsp olive oil
- 600g ground beef
- 1 onion, peeled and finely chopped
- 400ml beef stock – make sure it's gluten-free
- 100ml white wine or water – your choice
- 400g tin of butter beans, drain the can and rinse the beans
- 4 carrots, topped and tailed before being sliced
- 2 pieces of celery finely sliced
- Fresh herbs to taste – such as thyme or basil

Instructions

You can do this in a Dutch oven or over the hob

1. Step one is always to heat the oil. Simply place it in a pan over the hob
2. Add your onion and beef and then simmer for 15 minutes, stirring and turning regularly. The beef should go brown
3. Add your beef stock, wine (or water), and herbs
4. Bring the mixture to the boil then reduce the heat, cover, and leave for 45 minutes
5. Now add your beans, celery, and carrot
6. Recover the pot and cook on low heat for another 30 minutes, stirring halfway
7. Check the vegetables are tender, add any desired seasoning, and serve

Yellow Split Pea Soup

SERVES 5
PREP TIME: 10 MINUTES | TOTAL: 1HR 10 MINUTES
NET CARBS: 48G | PROTEIN: 21G | FIBRE: 15G | FAT: 24G
KCAL: 198

Ingredients

- 1 tbsp olive oil
- 1 onion peeled and finely chopped
- 2 pieces of celery finely sliced
- 3 crushed cloves of garlic
- 600ml vegetable stock
- 400g yellow split peas
- 1 potato, peeled and chopped into cubes
- 1 tbsp paprika powder
- 200ml cashew cream – or similar
- 2 tbsp apple cider vinegar

Instructions

1. Start by heating the oil in a standard pan over the stove
2. Put the onions and celery in the oil and sauté for approximately 5 minutes. The onion should be tender but not brown
3. Add the garlic and simmer for another minute
4. Now pour in your vegetable stock with the split peas, and paprika. Bring the mixture to the boil
5. Lower the temperature, allowing the soup to simmer for 45 minutes
6. Transfer the soup to a blender and blend until smooth
7. Add your cashew cream and apple cider vinegar while reheating
8. Serve with the garnish of your choice

Chilli Mushroom Soup

SERVES 8
PREP TIME: 15 MINUTES | TOTAL: 85 MINUTES
NET CARBS: 17G | PROTEIN: 21G | FIBRE: 3G | FAT: 23G
KCAL:364

Ingredients
- 2 tbsp olive oil
- 400g of sausages – you can use any type
- 400g ground beef
- 400g button mushrooms, any type can be used but they'll need to be cut into thin slices
- 1 tin tomato puree
- 400ml beef stock
- 1 tsp sugar
- Dash of Worcestershire sauce
- Pinch of garlic, oregano, and dried basil

Instructions

This soup is fantastic if made in a Dutch oven but, if you don't have one a standard pan will do

1. Start by putting the oil in a pan, or your Dutch oven and warming it.
2. Slice the sausages into thin slices and add them to the pan, along with the ground beef.
3. Simmer for 3-5 minutes until the pinkness has gone
4. Add your sliced mushrooms, tomato puree, beef stock, sugar, Worcestershire sauce, and the dried herbs – to your preferred taste
5. Turn the heat up and bring the soup to the boil, stirring as you do so
6. You can now turn the heat down, cover the pan and leave it to simmer for one hour. It's a good idea to stir a couple of times during the hour
7. Serve in bowls and enjoy

Lobster Delight

SERVES 6
PREP TIME: 15 MINUTES | TOTAL: 40 MINUTES
NET CARBS: 8G | PROTEIN: 8G | FIBRE: 2G | FAT: 12G
KCAL:228

Ingredients
- 1 tbsp olive oil
- 1 onion, peeled and chopped into small pieces
- 4 garlic cloves crushed
- 2 carrots – cut into thin slices
- 2 pieces celery – cut into thin slices
- 2 tbsp tomato puree
- 1 standard glass of white wine – you can choose which one
- 400ml vegetable stock
- 300ml cream
- 400g lobster meat – for speed buy lobster meat, not the lobster
- 2 tbsp butter
- 1 tbsp lemon juice

Instructions
1. Start by heating the olive oil in a pan over a medium heat
2. Once the oil is warm add the onions, garlic, celery, and carrots
3. Let them simmer for several minutes until they soften
4. Now add the tomato puree, vegetable stock, and your white wine
5. Bring the soup to the boil then turn the heat down, allowing it to simmer for 15 minutes
6. You'll now need to transfer the soup to a blender and blend it until smooth. This should only take a few minutes
7. Put the mixture back in the oven on a low heat
8. Separately, put your butter in a pan and warm it
9. Once melted add the lemon and you can add two crushed garlic cloves if desired
10. Add your lobster meat, cut it into small pieces, and cook for 3-4 minutes
11. Mix the mobster into the main soup and ensure it is piping hot before serving

Cheesy Taco Soup

SERVES '
PREP TIME: 10 MINUTES | TOTAL: 40 MINUTES
NET CARBS: 6G | PROTEIN: 5G | FIBRE: 5G | FAT: 16G
KCAL:279

Ingredients
- 2 tbsp olive oil
- 400g ground beef
- 1 green bell pepper – you'll need to chop it into small pieces
- 1 jalapeno – deseed it and chop it into small pieces
- 1 tin (400g) chopped tomatoes
- 400ml beef stock
- 1 small tin tomato puree
- 2 green chillies – deseeded and cut into small pieces
- A packet of taco seasoning
- 200g cream cheese
- 100ml cream

Instructions
1. Put the olive oil in a pan and warm it on the stove
2. Add the ground beef and simmer for 3-5 minutes. The aim is to eliminate the pinkness of the meat
3. Put your pepper, chopped tomatoes (with their juice), beef stock, tomato puree, taco seasoning, and the green chillies into the pan
4. Bring to the boil and then turn the heat down, allowing the soup to simmer for 20 minutes – it should thicken
5. Slowly mix in the cream and the cream cheese
6. Serve with your choice of garnish and accompaniment, you can blend it first if you wish for a smoother soup

French Onion Soup

SERVES 6
PREP TIME: 15 MINUTES | TOTAL: 2HRS 15 MINUTES
NET CARBS: 18G | PROTEIN: 10G | FIBRE: 2G | FAT: 22G
KCAL:319

Ingredients
- 4 onions peeled and sliced
- 100g butter
- 600ml beef stock
- 300ml water
- 2 cloves of garlic crushed
- 2 tsp coconut sugar
- 1 tsp dried thyme
- 100ml white wine
- 250g gruyere cheese – you can use other cheeses if you prefer
- Salt and pepper to taste

Instructions
1. Add a little of your butter to a pan and put it on the hob on a medium heat
2. Once melted, slide in the onions
3. Let the onions simmer for 4-5 minutes until they have softened
4. Mix in your coconut sugar, crushed garlic, and any salt or pepper you desire.
5. Now turn the heat down low and leave to simmer for 30 minutes, stirring occasionally
6. Tip the caramelized onions into a larger pan with the beef stock, water, wine, and thyme
7. Get the mixture to boiling point and then reduce the heat, allowing it to simmer for one hour
8. Check the taste and add extra salt, pepper, or any herbs to your preference
9. Serve while hot

WINTER SOUPS

Pesto Minestrone

SERVES 4
PREP TIME: 15 MINUTES | TOTAL: 55 MINUTES
NET CARBS: 28G | PROTEIN: 12G | FIBRE: 8G | FAT: 13G
KCAL:274

Ingredients
- 2 tbsp olive oil or similar
- 100g bacon –finely chopped
- 1 onion peeled and chopped
- 2 large carrots, topped and tailed then cut into small pieces
- 2 pieces of celery, also finely chopped
- 1 potato, peeled and chopped into cubes
- 2 crushed cloves of garlic
- 400g tin of chopped tomatoes
- 1l vegetable stock
- 400g tin of white beans, drained and rinsed
- 6 cabbage leaves grated or finely chopped

Instructions
1. Put a pan on the stove and add the oil, heat until it's warm
2. Add the onions and bacon and cook for 5 minutes, until the onions start to brown
3. Put the celery, carrots, garlic, and potato in and stir while cooking for another 3-4 minutes
4. Tip in the vegetable stock, ass the tomatoes and bring the soup to the boil
5. Reduce the heat and allow it to simmer, it's best to partially cover the pan
6. After 15 minutes add the cabbage and stir, continue simmering for another 15 minutes
7. While the soup is simmering, cut some fresh bread into chunks and put them in an ovenproof dish
8. Mix a little olive oil with a jar of pesto and make sure all the bread is coated, slide the tray into the oven and cook at 180°C for ten minutes
9. Now add the beans to the soup and simmer for an extra couple of minutes before serving with your pesto bread

The Indian Winter

SERVES 4
PREP TIME: 15 MINUTES | TOTAL: 45 MINUTES
NET CARBS: 58G | PROTEIN: 19G | FIBRE: 8G | FAT: 8G
KCAL: 445

Ingredients
- 100g pearl barley – that's standard barley with all the bran removed
- 2 tbsp olive oil
- 2 green chillies – you'll need to deseed them before chopping them into small pieces
- 1 onion peeled and cut into small pieces
- 2 cloves garlic – diced
- 1 parsnip – cut into small chunks
- 200g butternut squash – also chopped into cubes
- 200g sweet potato – chopped into small pieces
- 225g red lentils
- 2 fresh tomatoes – cut into sections
- 1 tsp lemon juice
- 1 tsp cumin seeds
- Pinch mustard seeds
- 2 cloves
- A stick of cinnamon
- Pinch ground turmeric
- Small piece of ginger root grated
- 1 tsp paprika

Instructions

1. Start by rinsing and cooking the pearl barley according to the instructions on the packet. Once cooked, drain it and put it to one side
2. Put your oil in a pan and heat on the stove
3. Add the mustard seeds, cumin, chillies, cloves, turmeric, and cinnamon
4. Cook gently until the seeds can be heard cracking
5. Add your onion and garlic, and cook for 5-6 minutes until they are soft
6. Now add the butternut squash, parsnip, and sweet potato. Keep stirring for several minutes to ensure the vegetables are fully coated and starting to soften
7. Add your paprika and ground seasoning and keep stirring
8. After a few minutes pour in the pearl barley, fresh tomatoes, and add 1.7 litres of boiling water
9. Bring the soup to the boil and reduce the heat, allowing it to simmer for 20 minutes
10. Add the ginger and lemon juice while on the heat
11. Remove and serve

Paprika, Red Pepper & Sweet Potato Soup

SERVES 2
PREP TIME: 10 MINUTES | TOTAL: 40 MINUTES
NET CARBS: 36G | PROTEIN: 9G | FIBRE: 8G | FAT: 33G
KCAL:491

Ingredients
- 2 tbsp olive oil or your preferred oil
- 1 large sweet potato – cut into cubes but leave the skin on
- 1 red pepper – remove the seeds and slice
- 1 onion – peeled and chopped into small pieces
- 3 cloves of garlic diced
- 200ml coconut milk
- 200ml chicken stock
- 1 tsp ground smoked paprika
- 1 tsp maple syrup - optional

Instructions
1. Turn your oven on to allow it to heat, 190°C or 170°C for a fan-assisted oven – Gas mark 5
2. Place the chopped sweet potato, peppers, onion, and garlic on an ovenproof tray
3. Sprinkle the paprika across the top and cover the vegetables in olive oil, making sure they are all coated
4. Slide the tray into the oven and cook for 30 minutes
5. Remove the vegetables and add them to your blender
6. Pour into the blender, with the vegetables, stock, coconut milk, and maple syrup, (if using)
7. Blend until the mixture is smooth
8. Pour the soup into a pan and heat on the stove
9. Serve when piping hot

Winter Lentil & Vegetable Soup

SERVES 2
PREP TIME: 10 MINUTES | TOTAL: 40 MINUTES
NET CARBS: 37G | PROTEIN: 16G | FIBRE: 13G | FAT: 3G
KCAL:264

Ingredients

- 2 carrots, topped and tailed then sliced lengthways
- 85g dried lentils, preferably red ones
- 3 pieces celery – cut lengthways
- 2 leeks – cut into thin circular pieces
- 2 tbsp tomato puree
- 3 cloves garlic peeled and diced
- 1 tbsp vegetable stock powder or one stock cube
- 2 tsp ground coriander
- 1 tsp dried thyme leaves if desired

Instructions

1. This couldn't be easier! Simply place all the ingredients in one pan
2. Add 1.5 litres of boiling water and put the pan on the hob while stirring
3. Set to low heat and allow it to simmer for 30 minutes
4. Serve and enjoy
5. If you want it thicker you can blend the soup and, if necessary, reheat it

Ultimate Winter Soup

SERVES 4
PREP TIME: 5 MINUTES | TOTAL: 25 MINUTES
NET CARBS: 34G | PROTEIN: 16G | FIBRE: 12G | FAT: 3G
KCAL:219

Ingredients
- 800g chopped tomatoes – 2 tins will suffice
- 5 carrots, topped and tailed then peeled and cut into thin slices
- 2 litres of vegetable stock
- 400g can red kidney beans – drained and rinsed in freshwater
- 400g white beans – also drained and rinsed in freshwater
- 200g spinach finely chopped
- 1 tbsp red pesto

Instructions
1. Make the vegetable stock with boiling water and pour it into a pan with the chopped tomatoes
2. Put the pan on high heat and bring the mixture to the boil
3. Turn the heat down and add your chopped carrots
4. Now allow it to simmer for 15 minutes
5. Add your red kidney beans and white beans, along with the spinach
6. Continue cooking for 5 minutes
7. Add the spoon of red pesto while stirring your soup
8. Make sure its hot right the way through before serving it with some fresh bread

Winter Vegetable

SERVES 4
PREP TIME: 5 MINUTES | TOTAL: 25 MINUTES
NET CARBS: 38G | PROTEIN: 17G | FIBRE: 14G | FAT: 7G
KCAL:307

Ingredients
- 1 tbsp olive or vegetable oil
- 4 carrots, topped and tailed then cut into pieces
- 2 crushed cloves of garlic
- 1 swede – peel it then cut it into cubes
- 850ml vegetable stock
- 500ml milk – semi-skimmed is fine or you can use full-fat
- 400g (1 tin) red kidney beans drained and rinsed
- 400g (1 tin) white beans drained and rinsed
- 2 tsp ground thyme

Instructions
1. Put your olive oil in a pan and set it on the hob over a medium heat
2. Once it is warm, add the garlic. Your aim is to soften it without changing its colour, 3-4 minutes should suffice
3. Add the carrots, 1tsp of thyme, and the swede
4. Gradually pour in the stock, stirring continually, then add the milk in the same way
5. Heat the mixture while stirring until it reaches boiling
6. Reduce the heat and allow to simmer for 15 minutes
7. Transfer the soup to your blender and blend until smooth
8. With the soup back in the pan, add the beans and any additional seasoning you desire
9. Heat thoroughly before serving

Hazelnut Truffle Soup

SERVES 6
PREP TIME: 20 MINUTES | TOTAL: 65 MINUTES
NET CARBS: 14G | PROTEIN: 5G | FIBRE: 11G | FAT: 15G
KCAL:237

Ingredients
- 1 tbsp vegetable or olive oil
- 1 onion, peeled and finely chopped
- 2 garlic cloves, peeled and chopped
- 800g celeriac
- 1 litre vegetable stock
- 50g hazelnuts – chopped into small pieces
- 1 potato – peeled and cut into large cubes
- 100ml soya cream
- 1 tbsp truffle oil
- Few thyme sprogs

Instructions
1. Put the oil in a pan and warm it on the hob over a medium heat
2. Drop the thyme in the pan with the onion and sauté for 10 minutes, stirring regularly. The onions should be soft not browned
3. Add your chopped garlic and sauté for another minute before adding the celeriac and potato cubes
4. Now add your vegetable stock and bring the soup to boiling point
5. Reduce the heat and half cover the pan as you leave it to simmer for 30 minutes
6. Pick the thyme out and get rid of it
7. Stir in the soya cream
8. Now remove the soup from the heat and transfer it to your blender, blend until smooth
9. Put it back in the pan and add your truffle oil while warming the soup
10. You may need to adjust the truffle oil depending on its strength and your taste buds
11. Once hot, serve and sprinkle the hazelnuts on top

Spicy Root Soup

SERVES 4
PREP TIME: 10 MINUTES | TOTAL: 45 MINUTES
NET CARBS: 34G | PROTEIN: 15G | FIBRE: 9G | FAT: 14G
KCAL:387

Ingredients
- 2 tbsp olive or vegetable oil
- 2 onions, peeled and thinly sliced
- 2 sweet potatoes – peeled and cut into cubes
- 2 carrots – topped and tailed then sliced
- 2 parsnips chopped into small pieces
- 1 tsp red chilli flakes
- 1 tbsp ground cumin
- 1.3 litres of vegetable stock
- 425ml semi-skimmed milk – you can use full-fat if you prefer
- 75g dried lentils – green is best for this recipe but red is okay
- 100g natural Greek yoghurt

Instructions
1. Put a pan on the stove and turn it on to medium heat, add the oil
2. After a minute drop the onion in and cook for 5 minutes, allowing the onions to soften
3. Now add the sweet potato, carrots, parsnips, cumin, and red chilli flakes, and allow them to sauté for another 7 minutes
4. Now pour the stock into your pan and tip in your dried lentils
5. Bring the mixture to the boiling point, reduce the heat, and simmer for 25 minutes
6. Transfer to the blender with the milk and blend until smooth
7. Add any additional seasoning then return the soup to the pan
8. Reheat, ensuring it is hot right through before serving
9. Once you've put it in the bowls put a spoonful of Greek yoghurt on the top

Cream of Cauliflower

SERVES 6
PREP TIME: 20 MINUTES | TOTAL: 40 MINUTES
NET CARBS: 43G | PROTEIN: 16G | FIBRE: 11G | FAT: 22G
KCAL:358

Ingredients

- 2 tbsp olive oil
- 1 cauliflower cut into small pieces
- 1 onion, peeled and finely sliced
- 3 cloves of garlic crushed
- 200g butter
- 250g flour
- 300ml milk – semi or full-fat will do
- 100ml whipping cream
- 600ml chicken stock
- 100g parmesan cheese - grated
- 3 tbsp ground parsley

Instructions

1. Turn your oven on, preheating it to 200°C, 180°C for fan-assisted, or gas mark 6
2. Place your garlic, cauliflower, and onion in a resealable freezer bag
3. Add the olive oil with a pinch of salt and pepper
4. Seal the bag and shake, ensuring the vegetables are evenly coated
5. Spread them on a clean baking tray and put them in the oven for 20-25 minutes
6. Separately, put the butter in a pan and melt it on medium heat on the hob
7. While heating, whisk the flour into your melted butter, the mixture should be smooth
8. Slowly add your milk, then the cream, and then the chicken stock, keeping the mixture smooth by whisking continually
9. Keep the heat low and stir as you bring it to boiling. Don't let it boil but simmer it to thicken the soup
10. Remove the roasted vegetables from the oven and mix them with the milk, then add the contents to your blender
11. Blend until smooth
12. Put it back in your pan and reheat for approximately 10 minutes, stirring regularly
13. Add the parmesan as you serve

Roasted Carrot And Ginger Soup

SERVES 6
PREP TIME: 10 MINUTES | TOTAL: 65 MINUTES
NET CARBS: 28G | PROTEIN: 5G | FIBRE: 8G | FAT: 5G
KCAL:149

Ingredients
- 1.5kg carrots – washed, topped and tailed, and sliced
- 2 tbsp olive oil
- 4 cloves of garlic finely chopped
- 1 litre of vegetable broth
- 250ml cream
- 1 piece ginger root, peeled and grated
- Salt and pepper to taste

Instructions
1. Turn your oven on and warm it to 200°C, that's 1800°C in a fan oven and gas mark 7
2. Spread the cut carrots on a baking tray and drizzle the olive oil across them. You can add some salt and pepper as well
3. Cook in the middle of the oven for 45 minutes
4. Remove and let cool
5. Place them in a blender with the ginger, half the stock, and your garlic, then puree them
6. Add the carrot mixture to a pan with the rest of the broth and any herbs or spices you wish to add
7. Bring it to the boil and allow it to simmer for 5 minutes
8. Reduce the heat and add the cream, stirring continuously
9. Now serve, if you wish you can garnish with fresh mint leaves

Beet Soup

SERVES 4
PREP TIME: 20 MINUTES | TOTAL: 60 MINUTES
NET CARBS: 17G | PROTEIN: 5G | FIBRE: 4G | FAT: 16G
KCAL:229

Ingredients
- 3 tbsp olive oil
- 1 onion, peeled and finely sliced
- 3 cloves of garlic – finely chopped
- 6 beetroots – peel them before chopping them into cubes
- 500ml beef stock
- 100ml heavy cream
- Salt and pepper to taste

Instructions
1. Put your olive oil in a pan on the stove and turn on medium heat, wait for it to melt
2. Add the onions and garlic then wait for them to soften. It should take 4-5 minutes
3. Add your beetroot cubes and cook for a further minute
4. Now pour in your beef stock and a little salt and pepper
5. Allow the mixture to boil before reducing the heat and covering
6. Leave it to simmer for 25-30 minutes
7. Transfer the soup to a blender and blend it until smooth
8. Before serving you may need to return it to the pan to reheat
9. Garnish with a little of the cream on each serving

Thai Green Curry Soup

SERVES 4
PREP TIME: 15 MINUTES | TOTAL: 30 MINUTES
NET CARBS: 27G | PROTEIN: 11G | FIBRE: 6G | FAT: 12G
KCAL: 284

Ingredients
- 1 packet of rice noodles
- 1 tbsp olive oil
- 700g chicken with bones removed, cut into small chunks
- 3 garlic cloves crushed
- 1 onion, peeled and diced
- 3 tbsp green curry paste
- 1 piece ginger root, peeled and grated
- 800ml chicken stock
- 200ml coconut milk
- 200g peas
- 2 tbsp lime juice
- 100g cilantro leaves – finely chopped

Instructions
1. Start by cooking the rice noodles, the instructions will be on the packet. Once cooked, drain and set aside
2. Put the olive oil in a pan and warm, add the chicken and season with salt and pepper
3. Mix in the garlic and onion then simmer for 5 minutes
4. Add the green curry paste and slowly blend in the ginger pieces while stirring on the heat
5. Now add your coconut milk and chicken stock
6. Turn the heat up to let the soup boil
7. Once boiling, reduce to low heat and let simmer for 15 minutes
8. Add your peas, cilantro, and lime juice and cook for a further minute
9. Serve with your noodles

FISH SOUPS

Prawn and Fennel Soup

SERVES 8
PREP TIME: 30 MINUTES | TOTAL: 55 MINUTES
NET CARBS: 7G | PROTEIN: 7G | FIBRE: 3G | FAT: 6G
KCAL:120

Ingredients
- 450g Tiger prawns in shells
- 4 tbsp olive oil
- 1 chopped onion
- 1 chopped fennel bulb
- 2 chopped carrots
- 150ml dry white wine
- 1 tablespoon Brandy
- 400g tin chopped tomatoes
- 1 litre fish stock
- 2 large pinches of paprika

Instructions
1. Heat the oil in a large pan
2. Shell the prawns and fry the shells for five minutes
3. Add the chopped onion, fennel and carrots
4. Cook for ten minutes
5. Add the wine and Brandy, stir well and cook for a further minute
6. Tip in the tomatoes, fish stock and paprika
7. Cover the pan and simmer for thirty minutes
8. Chop up the shelled prawns and put them to one side
9. Blend the soup mixture and then press it through a sieve
10. Pour this mixture back into a clean pan and add the chopped prawns
11. Cook for ten minutes
12. Blend again until smooth

Haddock and Sweetcorn Soup

SERVES 4
PREP TIME: 10 MINUTES | TOTAL: 20 MINUTES
NET CARBS: 43G | PROTEIN: 31G | FIBRE: 4G | FAT: 8 G
KCAL: 360

Ingredients
- 3 chopped medium potatoes
- 600ml full-fat milk
- 500ml fish stock
- 400g skinless smoked haddock fillet – cut into pieces
- 200g broccoli
- 2 x 198g tins of sweetcorn
- 2 sliced spring onions
- lemon juice

Instructions
1. Tip the potatoes into a large saucepan
2. Pour in the milk and fish stock
3. Bring to the boil then simmer for ten minutes
4. Gently mash some of the potatoes into the mixture
5. Add the haddock pieces and broccoli
6. Simmer for five minutes
7. Tip in the drained sweetcorn and a squeeze of lemon juice
8. Mix well and heat gently
9. Serve with a scattering of spring onions

Clam Chowder Soup

SERVES 6
PREP TIME: 15 MINUTES | TOTAL: 50 MINUTES
NET CARBS: 25G | PROTEIN: 17G | FIBRE: 5G | FAT: 14G
KCAL: 303

Ingredients
- 2kg clams
- 500g peeled and cubed potatoes
- 300g cubed parsnips
- ½ tablespoon olive oil
- 100g unsmoked bacon lardons
- 1 chopped onion
- 100g crème fraîche

Instructions
1. Add 1 litre of water to a large pan on a high heat
2. Once it is boiling, add the clams
3. Cover and cook for three minutes
4. Pour into a sieve over a large jug (to keep the cooking water)
5. Throw away any clams which have not opened
6. Remove ¾ of the clams from their shells and chop
7. Pour the cooking water from earlier through a muslin-lined sieve
8. Tip this into a large pan and add a bay leaf
9. Add the potatoes and parsnips and cook for seven minutes
10. Remove half the potato and parsnip and keep to one side
11. Remove the bay leaf and any scum from the water's surface
12. Blend the remaining mixture until smooth
13. Heat the oil in one of the empty pans
14. Add the lardons and fry until crispy
15. Remove and set aside
16. Add the onion to the pan and cook for five minutes
17. Pour in the blended mixture and add the potato and parsnip you put aside earlier
18. Heat until it is simmering
19. Tip in the chopped clams
20. Remove from the heat
21. Stir in the crème fraîche
22. Serve topped with the crispy lardons

Spicy Prawn Soup

SERVES 4
PREP TIME: 5 MINUTES | TOTAL: 20 MINUTES
NET CARBS: 32G | PROTEIN: 16G | FIBRE: 4G | FAT: 17G
KCAL: 327

Ingredients
- 300g stir fry vegetables
- 140g sliced shiitake mushrooms
- 2 tbsp Thai green curry paste
- 400g tin reduced-fat coconut milk
- 200ml vegetable or fish stock
- 300g medium straight-to-wok noodles
- 200g large raw prawns
- 1 tablespoon sunflower oil

Instructions
1. Heat a large wok and add the sunflower oil
2. Stir fry the vegetables and mushrooms for three minutes
3. Remove and place to one side
4. Add the Thai curry paste to the wok, fry for one minute
5. Pour in the stock and coconut milk
6. Bring to the boil
7. Add the noodles and prawns
8. Reduce the heat and simmer for four minutes
9. Tip in the vegetables and mushrooms
10. Stir well and serve

Sour and Hot Fish Soup

SERVES 4
PREP TIME: 15 MINUTES | TOTAL: 30 MINUTES
NET CARBS: 39G | PROTEIN: 29G | FIBRE: 1G | FAT: 7G
KCAL: 322

Ingredients
- 1 small piece of sliced ginger
- 1 teaspoon coriander seeds
- 850ml chicken or fish stock
- 175g thin rice noodles
- 2 tbsp fish sauce
- 2 deseeded and sliced red chillies
- 3 sliced garlic cloves
- 300g tail on tiger prawns raw
- 200g skinless salmon fillet cubed
- 4 chopped spring onions
- Few coriander leaves and mint leaves
- Lime juice

Instructions
1. Add the coriander seeds and ginger to a saucepan
2. Tip in the stock and bring to the boil
3. Simmer gently for five minutes
4. Leave to stand for ten minutes

Cook the noodles following the pack instructions
1. Drain and keep warm
2. Bring the stock mixture back to the boil
3. Tip in the fish sauce, chillies and garlic
4. Turn down the heat and simmer for two minutes
5. Add in the prawns and salmon
6. Return to a simmer and cook for five minutes
7. Add the spring onions, lime juice to taste and herbs
8. Share the noodles between the bowls
9. Lift out the prawns and salmon and add to the top of the noodles
10. Season the hot stock well and pour it into the bowls

Easy Fish Soup

SERVES 4
PREP TIME: 5 MINUTES | TOTAL: 15 MINUTES
NET CARBS: 5G | PROTEIN: 2G | FIBRE: 1G | FAT: 4G
KCAL: 143

Ingredients
- 2 crushed garlic cloves
- 1 tablespoon olive oil
- 1 teaspoon ground cumin
- ½ teaspoon paprika
- 200g tin chopped tomatoes
- 1 deseeded red pepper chopped
- 450g white fish fillets cut into pieces
- Roughly chopped coriander
- 1 lemon cut into wedges

Instructions
1. Heat the oil in a large pan
2. Add the crushed garlic, cumin and paprika
3. Cook for one minute
4. Pour in 100ml water and the chopped tomatoes
5. Bring the mixture to the boil
6. Turn down the heat
7. Tip in the pepper pieces, and simmer for five minutes
8. Add the fish pieces, and simmer for five minutes
9. Serve with coriander and a wedge of lemon

EXCLUSIVE BONUS

40 Weight Loss Recipes

&

14 Days Meal Plan

Scan the QR-Code and receive the FREE download:

Disclaimer

This book contains opinions and ideas of the author and is meant to teach the reader informative and helpful knowledge while due care should be taken by the user in the application of the information provided. The instructions and strategies are possibly not right for every reader and there is no guarantee that they work for everyone. Using this book and implementing the information/recipes therein contained is explicitly your own responsibility and risk. This work with all its contents, does not guarantee correctness, completion, quality or correctness of the provided information. Misinformation or misprints cannot be completely eliminated.

Printed in Great Britain
by Amazon